MW00398058

GRAND ENDEAVORS

Vintage Arizona Quilts and Their Makers

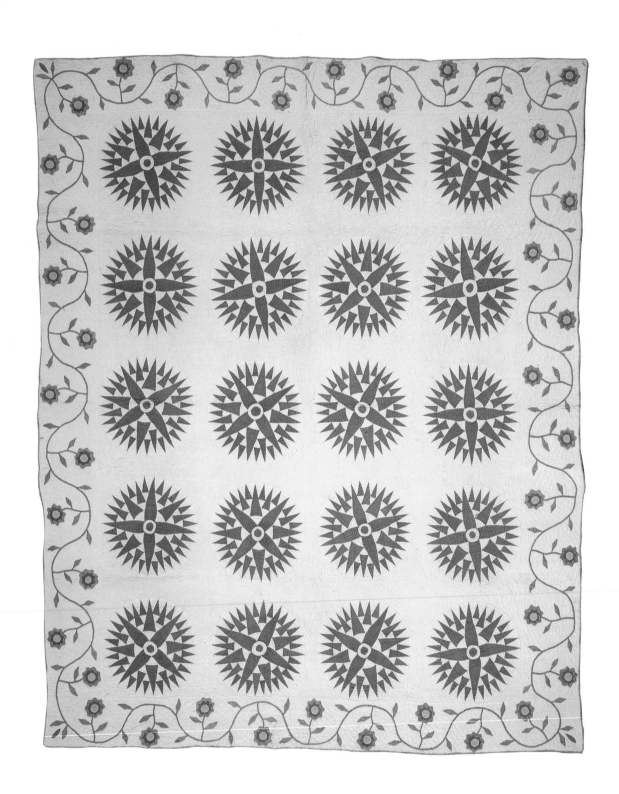

GRAND ENDEAVORS

Vintage Arizona Quilts and Their Makers

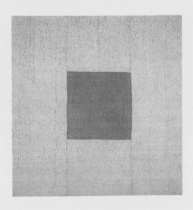

Helen Young Frost & Pam Knight Stevenson
Arizona Quilt Project

NORTHLAND
PUBLISHING

FRONTISPIECE: Mariner's Compass quilt by Mrs. Maffett, Tennessee, c. 1860; pieced and appliquéd cotton, 71" x 88." (see p. 154.)

Courtesy Carolyn S. Yost

Copyright © 1992 by the Arizona Quilt Project.

All rights reserved. This book may not be reproduced in whole or in part, by any means (with the exception of of short quotes for the purpose of review), without permission of the publisher. For information, address Northland Publishing Company, P.O. Box 1389, Flagstaff, Arizona 86002.

The information contained in this book was collected from a variety of sources, including oral histories. The authors have made every effort to verify its accuracy.

FIRST EDITION

ISBN: 0-87358-547-X

Library of Congress Catalog Card Number: 92-13929

Cataloging-in-Publication Data
Stevenson, Pam Knight.
    Grand endeavors : vintage Arizona quilts and their makers /
Pam Knight Stevenson & Helen Young Frost. -- 1st ed.
        216p.
    Includes bibliographical references and index.
    ISBN 0-87358-547-X (paperback) : $29.95
    1. Quilts --Arizona--History. 2. Quiltmakers --Arizona--Biography.
I. Frost, Helen Young. II. Title.
NK9112.S74   1992
746.9'7'09791--dc20   92-13929
                                                          CIP

Designed by Julie Sullivan Graphic Design
Manufactured in Hong Kong

9-92/7.5M/0369

*To Arizona pioneering women who inspire each
of us to our own grand endeavors*

THE ARIZONA QUILT PROJECT BOOK COMMITTEE

Val Benjamin
Janet Carruth
Helen Young Frost
Ruth Garrison
Diane Pitchford
Laurene Sinema
Pam Knight Stevenson
Audrey Waite

Edvardo Estrada Valdez VI standing in front of log cabin quilt c. early 1900s.

Courtesy Arizona Historical Society Library

TABLE OF CONTENTS

Sewing Bee in southern Arizona.

Courtesy Abijah Smith Collection, Arizona Historical Society Library

On a hot June day in 1986, thirteen women from different areas of Arizona gathered around a table laden with food and listened as a plan was unveiled—a plan that would foster grand friendships, a plan so far-reaching it would blanket an entire state and eventually touch many people in all parts of the world. Their love of quilts, their diverse talents, and their dedication to the plan were combined, and the Arizona Quilt Project was born. It was formed that day, with an endless enthusiasm, excitement, energy, and fortitude that would carry it through six years of intense dedication.

Quilts—their makers and owners, their designs and fabrics, their stories and their sheer beauty—kept fervor in the hearts of the project board.

A study of quilt projects in other states was made, and ideas from each one adapted to the special needs of Arizona. The Arizona Quilt Project was incorporated as a nonprofit Arizona Corporation. One of its first activities was to hold twenty-seven Quilt Discovery Days in twenty-six locations throughout the state.

People who owned quilts made in Arizona were encouraged to bring them to each Quilt Day. Those people possessing quilts of unknown origin, as well as quilts made elsewhere but now in Arizona, were also welcomed. The one criteria was that the quilts must have been made prior to 1940. Volunteers photographed the quilts, documented their physical characteristics, and recorded oral histories from the owners about the quilts and quiltmakers. The most historically significant quilt from each Quilt Day was chosen for a $100 award.

Each Quilt Day was a day of discovery for all those who participated: volunteers, quilt owners, quiltmakers, the project board, and individuals just passing by and observing. Board member Val Benjamin coordinated Quilt Day locations and volunteers. Over two years, a total of 2,774 quilts were documented.

The Arizona Quilt Project met monthly to review progress and to plan for the future. Meetings came alive, as people shared experiences and new ideas. From these sessions evolved an education program, a new video program, and this book.

An educational program called Quilt-Ed was implemented by board member Judy Schubert, with a committee that included teachers and quilters. Quilt-Ed assists teachers in using quiltmaking in their classrooms to teach history, art, language, math, writing, and vocabulary. A teacher's manual was written for fourth, fifth, and sixth grades. Training sessions were conducted by the Quilt-Ed committee and attended by teachers throughout Arizona. Over three years, more than 5,000 students participated by making quilts in their classrooms. Each spring an exhibit of student quilts was held at the Arizona State Capitol in Phoenix. *Quilter's Newsletter Magazine* and *Quilting Today* shared Quilt-Ed with their readers and, as a result, the Quilt-Ed teacher's manual has been sent to teachers around the world.

Board members Carole DeCosmo and Pam Stevenson produced a video program based on information gathered at Quilt Discovery Days. *Arizona Quilts: Pieces of Time* is a video program of stories about Arizona quiltmakers from territorial days to the present, told through quotes from letters, through historical photographs, and through interviews with quiltmakers and their families.

Fundraising was an enormous and necessary part of the Arizona Quilt Project. Innovative ideas were conceived and developed by board members Judy Schubert and Carole DeCosmo. A raffle quilt, four Small Quilt Auctions, and the sale of conservation materials, Quilt-Ed manuals, and the video all provided sources of income. Funds were also raised from corporate contributions, in-kind donations, and grants. Local and state quilt guilds and individual quilters were also generous with donations and support.

A book committee was formed before the Quilt Days were completed to begin the mammoth task of organizing the collection of information for publication. Headed by board member Janet Carruth, the committee reviewed every documented quilt to select those to be included in a book. A group of volunteers was trained to do additional research on selected quilts. The time-consuming and nerve-wracking task of bringing together one hundred and twenty-five quilts to be photographed professionally was coordinated by Diane Pitchford. Finally, two committee members, Helen Frost and Pam Stevenson, took the reams of research information and hundreds of photographs and transformed them into what would become this publication, *Grand Endeavors: Vintage Arizona Quilts and their Makers*.

Board member Penny Fowler, who headed the Exhibition Committee, worked with others to select a group of three hundred quilts from the more than three thousand quilts documented at Quilt Days; the final selection was made by out-of-state quilt experts who served as jurors. An extensive search resulted in two outstanding sites for our traveling exhibition: the Arizona State University Art Museum at the Nelson Fine Arts Center and the Arizona Historical Society Museum in Tucson. The combined efforts of all those involved have given the state a memorable exhibit, a fitting finale for the Arizona Quilt Project.

Additional dedicated board members include Audrey Waite, who served as secretary; Ruth Garrison, who edited our newsletter; Mary Beth Grosetta, who carried our quilt project message to communities throughout the state through her storytelling programs; and June Rector, our guardian angel, who was always behind the scenes filling in where needed.

The board joins me in expressing heartfelt thanks to our families. Not only did they support our time-consuming involvement in the project but husbands, children, extended family and friends allowed themselves to be volunteered for many assignments. Without them, our dream would not have materialized.

This book represents the culmination of six years of work. Within its covers, for everyone to enjoy, are both stories to be shared and visually interesting and beautiful photographs of the quilts and quiltmakers. We share with you our love of quilts and the opportunity these works of art offer us to know an important part of our American heritage.

Laurene Sinema
President, Arizona Quilt Project

The Arizona Quilt Project's two years of quilt documentation culminated in two exhibitions of outstanding quilts. The first showing of the exhibition, *Grand Endeavors: Vintage Arizona Quilts and Their Makers*, was held from November 8, 1992, until January 3, 1993, at the University Art Museum, Nelson Fine Arts Center, on the campus of Arizona State University in Tempe, Arizona. The exhibition then moved south to the Arizona Historical Society in Tucson, from January 15, 1993, until March 21, 1993.

Out of the nearly three thousand quilts that were documented at the twenty-seven Quilt Discovery Days, approximately fifty quilts were selected for the exhibition. The Exhibition Committee, headed by board member Penny Fowler, narrowed down the quilts to a more manageable group of about three hundred and fifty; and the final selection was made by three out-of-state quilt experts, who served as jurors. Jonathan Holstein from New York, Imelda DeGraw from Colorado (who also served as exhibit curator), and Cuesta Benberry from Missouri spent a long but fulfilling day making the final selections.

STATEMENTS FROM THE JURORS

Cuesta Benberry, a resident of St. Louis, Missouri, is a quilt historian. She has done extensive research on the African-American contribution to American quiltmaking and is particulary interested in slave-made quilts. Her pattern collecting started in the 1960s, and she graciously shares her knowledge and library of quilt reference material with anyone who asks. She is in demand around the country as a lecturer and consultant.

"A state quilt search project's primary objective is to discover and preserve the historical record of quilts within the state. Great emphasis is thus placed on locating quilts either made or owned by residents, hitherto unknown. Quilts are a visual medium, and a jurist needs to consider the aesthetic qualities of a quilt, as well as its historical significance. That was not a problem for us that day because numerous quilts of historical importance were also very graphic quilts. In fact, the Arizona Quilt Project had, in the slides presented to us, covered every possible eventuality.

"I had a special interest in a novelty quilt from Chandler. This quilt is composed of panels that showed African-Americans engaged in a late nineteenth-century dance, the "Cake Walk." Research revealed these panels were actually pillow covers, some manufactured by Campbell, Metzger, & Jacobson during a period when it was a custom to present black people as comic-derogatory stereotypes. The pillow covers were called "coon pillows" (coon was a contemptuous term applied to black people). Regardless of the manufacturer's intent in the 1880s, now, one hundred years later, we see a quilt that lost much of its pejorative connotations. Ironically, the quilt today is a vehicle for studying late Victorian-era fashions, a pictorial record of a popular pastime—the Cake Walk dance—and an undeniable late nineteenth-century historical artifact."

Imelda Gatton DeGraw, Curator of Textiles and Costumes at the Denver Art Museum, is well known to quilters as well as to museum professionals. She has, in her care, many treasured quilts and woven coverlets. Acquisition and exhibition of such a collection would not be possible without the interest and hard work of its curator. She has served in this capacity for several major exhibitions, here and abroad.

"The objective of a juried exhibition is to have the most comprehensive presentation possible. This means not only quality in the objects selected but also an interesting mix of subject matter, so as to present a stimulating visual experience for the visitors to the exhibition. Many utilitarian examples were a reminder of the economic hardships endured by the women who strived to make the home comfortable and beautiful by their piece making. We viewed slides of these memory transmitters, not fully aware of the fragility of the textiles—many of which had passed the age of 100. Intricate quilting stitches are seldom visible in slide presentations. Is the appliqué exquisite? Masterful piecing is denoted by diamond shapes coming point-to-point. Triangles in perfect harmony and squares meticulously perfect are other elements to evaluate. Visual triumphs often contributed to the final decision. Thanks to the wealth of beautiful Arizona-owned quilts, we were to achieve the goals set forth."

Jonathan Holstein grew up around American decorative arts in upstate New York. This fostered a lifelong interest in Americana and Native American Art. He and his wife, Gail van der Hoof, collected visually exciting quilts and set in motion the current boom in quiltmaking with their landmark 1971 quilt exhibit at the Whitney Museum of Art in New York City. Jonathan's book, *The Pieced Quilt: An American Design Tradition,* has become an invaluable resource for those who appreciate and collect quilts.

"The 370 quilts they presented to us for consideration could have made a number of wonderful exhibitions. There were some wonderful surprises, among which were a number of superb early high-style quilts (broderie perse and Baltimore style album quilts, an 1832 central medallion quilt with hearts and flower vases, an extraordinary linsey-woolsey quilt with a cochineal red square floating in a mustard field). These are clearly treasured heirloom quilts brought to the state either by early settlers seeking land or later ones seeking the sun. There were a large number of aesthetically amazing pieced quilts, including some in very small, and others in very large and bold, patterns, and a remarkable crazy quilt in squares. I am also haunted still by the strange and triumphant mosaic masterpiece which looks like a weaving diagram and has the cryptic word, "Orientel," at the bottom. All these wonders, and others, are part of this exhibition, whose quality is a tribute to the patience and extraordinary effort of those who planned, ran, and aided the Arizona Quilt Project."

In the 1860s, Arizona was unknown to most Americans. Those who were aware of it imagined a land of scorching, barren desert and hostile Indians. Its cool pine forests, mighty rivers, and grand geologic wonders were still known only to a relative few. To the east, the United States flourished as the Industrial Revolution advanced. To the west, California boomed with prosperity of the Gold Rush and recent statehood.

In 1853, the Spanish pueblo of Tucson and a long narrow strip of land running east to west had been added to the United States as part of the Gadsden Purchase from Mexico. It was not until 1863, however, that Arizona officially become a U.S. Territory separate from New Mexico.

It was a brave woman who ventured into the Arizona Territory. Usually the wife or daughter of a rancher, a farmer, a miner, or a soldier, she raised a family, organized a church and started a school, while he worked to build a business, find a fortune or protect settlers. She brought to Arizona all the skills she had learned from her mother and grandmother. In addition to raising children, she grew a garden, canned fruits and vegetables, tended chickens, churned butter, and milked the family cow. She knew how to cut wood, haul water, and use a gun. She also sewed the family's clothes and made bedding to keep them warm at night. The adage, "a woman's work is never done" was never more true than for pioneer Arizona women.

Making do with what she had was not new. These hardy women drew from experience passed on to them by generations of women, and quilting was an important part of this tradition. When cloth was scarce, women made use of every scrap, sewing together bits and pieces of familiar cloth to make warm bed covers. Frequently not content to simply sew these scraps together, they stitched the pieces into patterns, they shared the patterns with friends, and over the years, gave them names. Maryland became known for the "Baltimore Album," Texas for the "Lone Star." Women fighting for the abolition of alcohol stitched "Drunkard's Path."

These colorful quilts added a spot of brightness to the women's homes and to their lives. And, unlike most of the daily chores that filled a woman's life, the "work" of making a quilt rewarded her with a tangible creation that could be used, admired, and even passed on to future generations.

Expected to help supply the family with clothing and bedding, young girls were taught basic sewing skills at an early age. Making a sampler, with cross-stitched alphabets and perhaps a verse or scripture, taught both the basic embroidery skills and the alphabet. There was no better exercise, however, for learning to sew a fine seam than the piecing of squares into patchwork. Girls as young as three learned to ply a needle by joining scraps into a four-patch or nine-patch that could be used as a small quilt for their favorite doll or perhaps as the first block of the many needed for a bed quilt. They also learned practical lessons about patience and perseverance.

The patenting of Elias Howe's sewing machine in 1856 signalled the beginning of a new era for quilts; many quilts from that time have some machine stitching, which demonstrates a quick acceptance of the new timesaving device. Small pieces were usually still joined by hand, but longer seams such as those connecting blocks, were more and more frequently sewn by machine.

Quilts reflect changes in the fabrics of fashion, styles in dec-

William and Josephene Speed, in front of their home in Willcox, AZ, c. 1900.

Courtesy Arizona Historical Society Library

orating, and fads in needlework, as well as characteristics of the era in which they were made. So distinct were some of the changes, including developments in fabric dyeing and printing, that most quilts can be reliably dated a century or more after their creation.

Ultimately, Arizona drew women from all corners of the nation, and they brought with them patterns and quilts from their home towns. Quilts came to Arizona from every region of the country, and virtually every major type or style was represented. Because of Arizona's relatively recent settlement, and its sunny appeal to those seeking renewed health or retirement, an overwhelming number of the quilts documented by the Arizona Quilt Project were made elsewhere. The wide variety of quilts make it possible to trace many of the trends and traditions of quiltmaking.

Quilts were used to celebrate and commemorate; special people or special events were traditionally honored with quilts. Quilts have also long served as a means of creative self-expression. Quilt artisans used their eye for beauty and design along with their needlework skill to take quiltmaking beyond its practical purpose into the realm of art.

The women and quilts of Arizona reflect a blending of traditions from all parts of America and the world. Their quilts were both simple, warm, bedcovers and meticulously stitched fabric art. The women who made Arizona home before 1940 came to a frontier and stayed to raise families and build communities. Both the lives these women led and the quilts they made were Grand Endeavors.

Mary Smith, age 19, Harvey House Girl in Las Vegas, New Mexico, 1892.

Courtesy Mrs. John W. Lawler

WITNESS TO HISTORY

Arizona's Past Seen Through Quilts

Detail of center of block in Pineapple quilt with embroidered gold key by Atanacia Santa Cruz Hughes.

Courtesy Arizona Historical Society Library

Quilts made by Arizona women reflect the diversity of the state, the people of all backgrounds, from all parts of the world, who chose to make Arizona their home. They also reflect the places they chose to settle: southern Arizona communities that share a heritage with Mexico; desert cities that were created through technology that brought them water; settlements carved out of pine forests that share their natural wonders with visitors from around the world. Arizona quilts reflect this diversity, while sharing threads common to all quiltmakers.

HISPANIC HERITAGE

Tucson, Arizona, began as a sleepy Indian village. In 1776, it became a walled Spanish city, and, a century later, a U.S. military outpost. Then, in the spring of 1880, the arrival of the Southern Pacific Railroad transformed Tucson into a key business and supply center.

> *"I do not remember ever having seen a less inviting, less promising prospect for a home. Tucson is certainly the most forlorn, dreary, desolate, Godforsaken spot on earth."*
>
> MINA OURY
> 1865 Diary

The U.S. census of 1860, the first taken in Arizona Territory, listed only forty-four women over the age of sixteen; of those, twenty-nine lived in the Santa Cruz River Valley between Tucson and the Mexican border. Most were probably Mexican women. The Anglo-American men who ventured into Arizona Territory were young and single. They came seeking fortune and adventure, or sometimes fleeing justice. Some were sent by their employers, usually mining companies, mail companies, or the U.S. Army. Many were attracted to the beauty and charm of the native Mexican girls and made them their wives.

Such was the case of Atanacia and Petra Santa Cruz. Born in Tucson in 1850, when it was still part of the Mexican state of Sonora, Atanacia was orphaned and living with her older sister Petra and her husband, Hirum Stevens, when at the age of eight, she first saw the man who would someday become her husband.

Samuel Hughes was almost thirty years old when he arrived in Tucson on a sunny March day in 1858. Born in Wales, Samuel Hughes came to Arizona by way of the California gold fields. Charmed by the warm climate and the friendly Spanish people, he became a dealer in grain and livestock, supplying the stage stations between Maricopa Wells and Apache Pass.

The stage line, established in 1858 by the Butterfield Company, carried the overland mail as well as passengers. The trip from St. Louis to San Francisco took an average of twenty-four days. Westward-bound passengers paid two hundred dollars, eastward bound only one hundred dollars; the fare included an allowance for forty pounds of baggage. Meals were served at the stage stations at prices ranging from seventy-five cents to a dollar, amounts that generated a great deal of complaint. Sam Hughes later wrote of that business venture, "I

ABOVE: *Atanacia Santa Cruz Hughes,*
Samuel Hughes, and daughter Lizzie,
c. 1866, San Francisco, California. Lizzie
was her third child; her first two baby boys
had died at birth. Atanacia had a total of
15 children, 9 lived to be adults.
Courtesy Arizona Historical Society Library

LEFT: *Pineapple quilt by Atanacia Santa*
Cruz Hughes (1850–1934) Tucson,
Arizona, 1884; pieced silk with embroi-
dered flowers and symbols, 72" x 62."
Collection of Arizona Historical Society, Southern
Arizona Division Museum

made money hand over fist until the war broke out." Even in the remote Arizona Territory, the routine of life and business was disrupted by the outbreak of the Civil War. The U.S. Army recalled soldiers protecting Arizona settlements, American settlers chose sides, and many hastily departed. In February 1862, Confederate President Jefferson Davis officially proclaimed Arizona a Confederate Territory. Later that month, a Confederate company arrived in Tucson. They were welcomed by the mostly Mexican townspeople, who had felt abandoned and vulnerable to Apache attacks when the U.S. troops left for Civil War duty in the East.

Told to take an oath of allegiance to the Confederacy or leave, Sam Hughes, a Republican and strongly pro-Union, chose to leave. He went to California and returned in May with the Union's California Column. The Confederates evacuated Tucson before the arrival of 2,300 men in blue.

Upon his return, Hughes noticed that Atanacia Santa Cruz had become a lovely young lady. At first, Atanacia resisted his offer of marriage because she didn't know how to cook or do laundry. She had led a sheltered life and been taught the gracious manners of a Mexican lady, including the skills of fine sewing and embroidery. Sam promised she would never have to worry about these domestic chores, and in 1862, at age

twelve, she married the thirty-three-year-old Sam Hughes.

Her wedding took place at the Mission San Xavier Del Bac, five miles south of Tucson. The mission was founded in the late seventeenth century under the direction of Father Kino; Atanacia's great-grandfather had helped paint the murals that cover the walls inside the sanctuary. For her wedding Atanacia wore a black taffeta silk dress trimmed with ruffles and a black lace mantilla. She wanted to wear white but an aunt insisted on black since "a wedding was a serious thing and just as solemn as a funeral." It may also have been considered inappropriate to wear white because Sam Hughes was not a Catholic.

Sam was busy re-establishing his business, so there was no time for a honeymoon. But in 1866, Sam fulfilled a promise and took Atanacia on a belated wedding journey to San Francisco. They traveled by wagon to Guaymas in Sonora, Mexico; from there they went by ship to San Francisco, and then once again by wagon down the California coast, visiting Monterey, Los Angeles, and San Diego.

This trip opened a new world to the young girl from Tucson. When they returned to Tucson after two years, Atanacia brought with her a new baby, her fourth child (her first two babies died at birth, and a small daughter accompanied them on their wedding journey). She also brought a gift

Sam had purchased in San Francisco. Such a device had never been seen before in Tucson and all the women came to the Hughes home to admire this wonderful invention. It was a Singer sewing machine.

For a time in the early 1880s, Atanacia and four of her children went to live in Lawrence, Kansas, so the children could attend school; at the time, schools in Tucson were rudimentary at best. In Kansas, Atanacia learned to speak, read, and write English, and it was also probably in Kansas that she was introduced to the American tradition of patchwork quilting.

Atanacia was known for her fine needlework, and Arizona's blending of cultures is represented by a silk quilt she made in 1884. Stitched in a traditional Pineapple pattern, and decorated with Mexican symbols and words, the quilt's blocks contain a center square embroidered with flowers, religious symbols, or Spanish words. Some of the symbolism remains a mystery, but it loosely translates to "We married at a holy time. We became a faithful family. One key guides us in a straight line." The fourth, fifth, and sixth rows translate as "I do not offer, nor give myself to anyone but my master." (The word, "master" could be a reference to God, or to her husband.) The initials, A.H., are those of the maker, Atanacia Hughes.

The same year the Pineapple quilt was made, 1884,

An accomplished musican,
Atanacia Hughes played the harp in the
early 1900s, Tucson, Arizona.
Courtesy Arizona Historical Society Library

Atanacia's husband met with Charles D. Poston to organize the first meeting of the Arizona Pioneers Society. Sam, by now a successful butcher and merchant, spent ten dollars for paper and envelopes to write the "men who came and meant to stay," inviting them to join. Several years later, he served as president of the society, forerunner of the Arizona Historical Society. Together, the Hughes played an important role in the "civilizing" of Tucson. They helped to found churches and schools (both Catholic and Protestant), and Sam served as an alderman, sheriff, county treasurer, and adjutant general of Arizona Territory. Atanacia eagerly and proudly cast her first ballot in 1914, the first election in which women could vote. A great granddaughter remembers Atanacia as quiet, but always firmly in charge. "If you were naughty, she thumped you on the head with her thimble. But afterward she'd slip a lemon drop into your hand."

Like Atanacia Hughes, Manuela Sosa McKenna was also proud of her family's Spanish heritage. Manuela Sosa was a small child in the 1850s when her family moved north to Tucson from Santa Ana, Sonora. On January 20, 1867, when she was fourteen, Manuela married Michael McKenna. He was fifteen years her senior, had already led an exciting life as a soldier in the Mexican–American War, was a successful Tucson

merchant, and a legislator in the Third Territorial Assembly. Manuela recorded her marriage and the birth dates of her husband, herself, and seven of her twelve children on a unique embroidered quilt. On the bottom row she included her maiden name, "Sosa," important in Spanish culture where children often retain the family names of both parents.

Manuela constructed the quilt to be hung on a wall. It is made of a single layer of rectangular blocks of wool suiting fabrics. The names and dates are delicately embroidered and embellished with French knots. Blocks between the names and dates are embroidered with birds and flowers, and buttonhole stitching finishes the unusual scalloped edging. Manuela is said to have made this family record during an illness of her husband. It was carefully passed down through the family and, in 1953, was donated to the Arizona Historical Society by a granddaughter living then in San Francisco.

ABOVE: Manuela Sosa and Michael McKenna, wedding photo, 1867, Tucson, Arizona.
Courtesy Arizona Historical Society Library

LEFT: McKenna Genealogy quilt made by Manuela Sosa McKenna (1852–1907) Tucson, Arizona, circa 1890; pieced wool elaborately embroidered with family names and birth dates, 60" x 89."
Collection of Arizona Historical Society, Southern Arizona Division Musuem

OPPOSITE: Detail of center block, embroidered with the marriage date of Manuela Sosa and Michael McKenna.

HARDY PIONEERS

While Atanacia and Manuela were raising their families in the old pueblo of Tucson, to the north a number of small communities were beginning to gain a foothold in the Arizona Territory. When Abraham Lincoln officially declared Arizona a territory in 1863, there was suspicion that Tucson was still sympathetic to the Confederate cause. The territorial capitol was therefore located in the tiny central-Arizona mining town of Prescott. One of the first Anglo women to venture into that rugged community was Mary Ritter. The Ritters first traveled through Arizona in 1863 on their way from Texas to California. They settled on a ranch in California and according to family stories, Mary Ritter was warned one day by an Indian woman she had befriended that there would be an uprising. Mary insisted the family go into San Diego for safety, and that night Indians killed everyone in the area and burned anything that would burn.

As the story continues, her husband Jacob fondly recalled an area they had traveled through in Arizona, a place where the grass was high and beautiful on the gently rolling hills and the sun was warm. They packed up their remaining belongings and returned to that spot, west of Prescott, in 1868.

The Ritter family established a ranch along the Ehrenberg wagon road, the main route between Prescott and the Colorado River. They raised cattle and sold fresh fruits and vegetables from Mary's large garden to travelers along the road.

Mary and Jacob had twelve children, but only seven grew to adulthood. In 1905, she made a blue-and-white Log Cabin quilt as a wedding gift for her son Ed and his bride. The simple cotton fabrics are arranged in a dramatic setting with a red center block symbolizing the hearth of the home. Mary died in 1911, before her grandson Curtis was born, but when he received the quilt, it still had a small note attached that read "This quilt was made for Ed Ritter by his mother to give to his son." Curtis Ritter treasures the quilt that ties him to the grandmother he never knew.

As life in the Arizona Territory became more settled, more and more women arrived to civilize rough Arizona towns. Their quilts wrapped newborns and cushioned the bumps in covered wagons. They were a link to families left behind, often never to be seen again.

Quilts often also recorded family and community history. Martha Alice Lawson Hunter gave her son such a quilt when he headed west to Arizona in 1866. Thomas Thompson

ABOVE: Mary Jane Chowning Ritter, late 1800s.
Courtesy Phoebe Ritter

LEFT: Log Cabin quilt, Courthouse Steps variation, made by Mary Ritter (1842–1911) Hillside, Arizona, c. 1905; pieced cotton, quilted all over with an ocean wave pattern, 62" x 77."
Courtesy Phoebe Ritter

Hunter enlisted in the Confederate Army at the tender age of sixteen. After the war, he returned home to his parents' plantation in Louisiana, and then joined an uncle and a party of emigrants bound for Texas. With Thomas went a very special original quilt made up of thirty blocks, each one with seven tiny, red, six-pointed stars, pieced and appliquéd on the center and six points of a compass. The white background was then elegantly quilted.

Also traveling in the group was William Gallaspy, a former Confederate captain, and his sixteen-year-old daughter, Ollie Elizabeth. Somewhere en route, Thomas Hunter decided to continue farther west; he also found himself falling in love with Ollie Elizabeth Gallaspy. The Gallaspy party entered Arizona Territory in the fall of 1867. Thomas later wrote, "The trip was a dreary one from the start, accompanied with dangers and hardships innumerable. Every inch of the distance achieved was menaced with hostile Indians, who never lost an opportunity to attack our outfit. Apache Pass was the first place reached in Arizona of any note. A small command of U.S. Infantry occupied the military post there, known as Fort Bowie. On the day of our arrival at Bowie, it looked pretty gloomy and lonesome for the few soldiers stationed there."

Thomas and Ollie Elizabeth were married in Wickenburg,

the first marriage recorded in the fledgling mining town. After two years in Arizona, the Hunters continued on to California. They later returned to the Arizona Territory in 1878 with three young daughters and settled in Cochise County, where they established a successful cattle business and had one more daughter. In 1885, Thomas Hunter was elected to serve in the Thirteenth Territorial Legislature, also called the "Thieving Thirteenth" by those citizens who objected to the body's overspending and excessive travel allowances. Martha Hunter's unusual Seven Stars quilt survived these frontier travels, and has been passed down through three generations.

In the late 1870s, a new wave of settlers began to sweep across Arizona. Unlike many earlier adventurers, they were not seeking fortunes or excitement, but simply homes for their families and freedom of religion. Most came from the north; they crossed the Grand Canyon and the Colorado River, following the Little Colorado east and south and establishing small farming and ranching communities along the way.

To the north of Arizona was the neighboring territory of Utah, settled in 1847 by Brigham Young and devoted members of the Church of Jesus Christ of Latter-day Saints. Driven from their homes in Illinois and Missouri, they found refuge in the Salt Lake Valley. This was their Zion, so-called after the ideal-

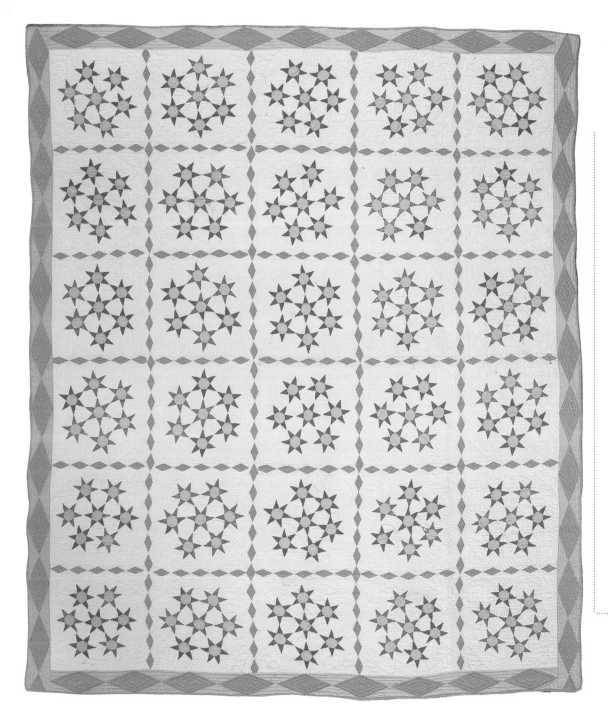

LEFT: Seven Stars quilt, Martha Alice Lawson Hunter, Louisiana, c. 1860; pieced and appliquéd cotton, 79" x 91."

Courtesy Agnes Lambert

ized national homeland of the Jews in the Old Testament. As thousands of new members, converted through worldwide proselytizing efforts, streamed into Salt Lake City, they were often "called" or chosen by Brigham Young to settle outlying areas of Utah. After John D. Lee established a ferry crossing the Colorado River in 1872, Mormons, as they were also known, were sent to establish homes, farms, and ranches in Arizona. These settlers, often as newlyweds, were some of the first Anglo-Americans to come to Arizona as families. The women brought with them their family quilts and a long tradition of quilting.

The devoutly Mormon Weech family came to Arizona in 1878. Sarah Dall Weech drove a horse team attached to a spring wagon, while her husband Hyrum drove two yoke of oxen hitched to the supply wagon. Sarah later recalled: "It was quite a task for me to drive the team and care for six children, but I got along very well."

She also recorded an incident that occurred in their camp during the trip, while the men were away. "The children were playing near the rock when suddenly some Indians appeared. They proved to be friendly, and so we were not harmed, but to the children I was a heroine and saved their lives." After three months of travel, they were among the first settlers to arrive in

Smithville in southeastern Arizona. Hyrum helped to lay out the town that would come to be called Pima.

Sarah Dall was born in England in 1849. When she was six, she came with her family to the United States and gathered with other Mormons in Utah. The family settled in Goshen, Utah, in 1858, and it was there that Sarah learned to spin and weave. Sarah recalled that at the age of nine, "I herded the sheep, carded the wool, spun it into yarn, dyed it, and wove it into the cloth from which my first woolen dress was made. I also helped in making it."

Sarah received only a week of schooling, since the twenty-five cent weekly fee was more than her family could afford. At age seventeen, she married Hyrum Weech. When Sarah needed some dresses following the birth of her first child the following year, Hyrum pawned one of his pistols for the money for the cloth. At the time, calico was sixty cents per yard; lawn was a dollar twenty-five. It wasn't until they were the parents of six children, all born in Utah in the log house that was their first home, that the Weech family bought a cooking stove. They also purchased one of the first sewing machines on the market, a Howe, for one hundred and fifteen dollars, for which they paid in hay. Of their early life, Sarah recalled, "I used to knit all the stockings for myself and family, also knitted and crocheted lace

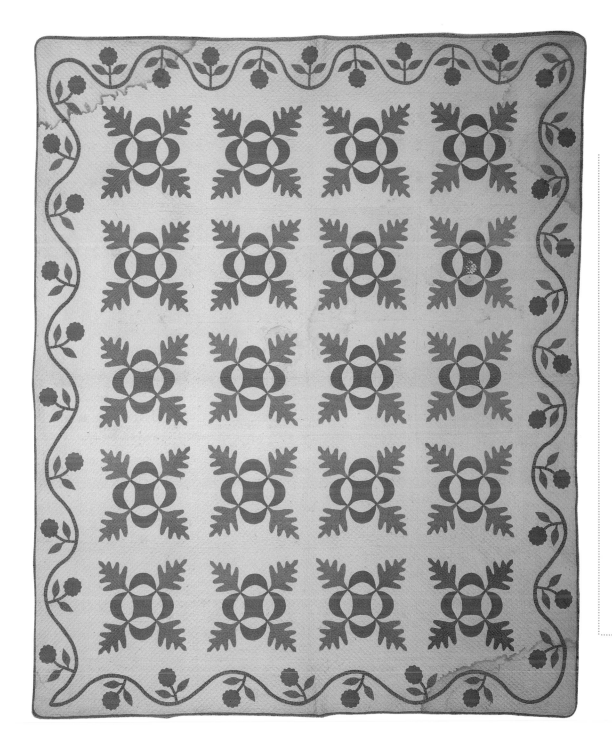

Oak Leaf & Reel quilt made by Weech family, Utah, c. 1850; appliqué, 81" x 98."

Collection of Eastern Arizona Historical Society

to trim our underclothes, and our pillowcases. Most of our hats were home-made also. They were made of straw which I prepared, braided and fashioned myself. I was always busy." To make extra money for the family Sarah also sold handmade lace and did quilting for others.

Sarah brought her Howe sewing machine and her treasured Oak Leaf and Reel quilt with her to Arizona. The traditional red-and-green appliqué design displays expert workmanship and must surely have been saved for special occasions.

For the first year, their Arizona home was the tent they brought with them. "We had only the ground for a floor and our first table was made of four posts driven into the ground and a dry goods box turned over them, the bottom of the box forming the top of the table."

While living in their new community, the Weechs built a log house, one end of which was to be used as a store. They could not afford windows or the lumber for doors, so the family hung quilts over the doorways and used muslin for window coverings. Supplies for the store were purchased in Tucson. Sarah later recalled that prices were so high that several women would buy one package of baking soda and she would measure it out by the spoonsful. Thread was twenty-five cents a spool. Sarah wrote, "my husband had to make frequent trips to

Tucson for goods for the store as there was no railroad then, not even to Tucson. He had to travel alone, and every time that he went I did not know whether or not I would see him alive again. The Indians were killing people all around us, and there was a band of rustlers who were stealing horses most of the time from travelers and ranchers. My husband was liable to lose his horse any night while on these trips, or he might be killed by Indians. So one can imagine what my state of mind was."

To prepare for a visit from her sister and family, who were also moving to Arizona, Sarah whitewashed the walls of the log house, then covered the dirt floor with hay and a rag carpet. Sarah later recalled, "When the job was finished, I felt quite proud of our home. Well, my sister and family arrived and after looking around a while my sister said, 'Well, Sarah, I never did see you live in such a dirty house.' I told her to just wait until she had lived in Arizona a year and we would see how nice and clean her home would look."

The history of an entire community was recorded in another quilt that "headed West" to Arizona. In 1882, Jane Nugent Hart was preparing to leave Wisconsin to join her husband "Lum" in Tombstone, where he made his living as a gunsmith. Surprised one evening by a knock at the door, Jane opened it to friends and neighbors who had come to bring a farewell gift,

Jane Nugent Hart and Samuel "Lum" Lumbard Hart c. 1880
Courtesy Ed and Dee King

a Friendship Album quilt. A simplified Chimney Sweep pattern, the center of each block of the quilt contains ink signatures of friends and neighbors who hoped to be remembered. Several also have special poems. One reads:

Remember Jane and bear in mind
A good true friend is hard to find.
And when you find one just as true
Change not the old one for the new.

June 20th 1881 Oll. V. Sarah

The quilt was machine quilted in an allover grid. (Perhaps the makers of the quilt were hurrying to finish their surprise gift.) In a letter (right) to her husband, Jane described the visit. This letter, with its prophetic message, has been preserved with the quilt by the great-grandson of Lum and Jane Hart.

When Jane Hart arrived, Tombstone was barely four years old and had already begun to earn the reputation that would make it famous. One can only speculate what Jane and her Wisconsin friends must have imagined of a town named Tombstone.

*ear Husband,*

There has been a raid on the house. I was sitting very quietly
knitting when in walked 36 of the citizens with their supper.
I felt weak in the knees, then after supper they
presented me with an Album quilt with all the old names...
I wish you could see it.

(Greetings from their friends were added to the back of the letter...)

"Lum,
I love you as well as ever & only wish you were here
to enjoy this evening with us. Jane is on her knees (not praying)
looking over the album quilt."
"House full noise the principal music."
"Lum you don't know how much we missed you tonight.
We missed your stories and jokes."
"May this paper with this scribly long be preserved."

When founder Ed Schieffelin began to prospect in the desolate Mule Mountains, he was warned he would only find his tombstone. Instead, he found rich deposits of silver. In its heyday, the boomtown of Tombstone claimed the greatest population of any town between New Orleans and San Francisco. A young actress, Josephine Marcus, visiting Tombstone in 1880, wrote: "The hill south of town was crawling with mining activity. The sound of machinery came from there day and night. By then there were even regular shifts, with whistles to signal the start and finish of them. Tombsone was getting to be a regular city."

Among that population were reckless adventurers and outlaws from justice. The Tombstone jail was a prominent spot in town, and the job of sheriff was not an easy one to fill. When Jerome Lemuel Ward became the sheriff of Cochise County in 1882, the famous incident at the OK Corral involving the Earp brothers and Doc Holliday was just a year in the past. His oldest son, Will J. Ward, was deputy sheriff and served as jailor.

According to family stories, while a troupe of entertainers was playing at the Bird Cage Theatre in Tombstone, a distur-

bance arose in the audience. The husband of one of the actresses went to investigate and a shot was fired. The whole troupe was jailed as material witnesses.

While she was in jail, one actress tore up some of her clothes to make this pink-and-blue Log Cabin baby quilt for Deputy Will Ward's wife Jennie, who was expecting a child. Blue-and-white silk gingham strips may have come from the unknown actress's dress; the pink silk strips from her camisole; and the white wool challis from her petticoat. The baby, the Wards' second daughter, was born December 9, 1883, and was named Belle.

By the late 1880s, the wild element of Tombstone was greatly reduced by the presence of Cochise County Sheriff John Slaughter. Former Confederate soldier and Texas Ranger, Sheriff Slaughter told outlaws to "get out or get killed." So conscientious was he that the Tombstone jail, overflowing with prisoners, was dubbed the "Hotel de Slaughter."

Slaughter brought his family and several hundred head of cattle from Texas to Arizona in 1878. When his wife died in Phoenix that same year, he was left with two small children. It was while John Slaughter was in New Mexico the following year, awaiting more of his cattle from Texas, that he married Cora Viola Howell.

The daughter of former slaveholders from Missouri, Viola

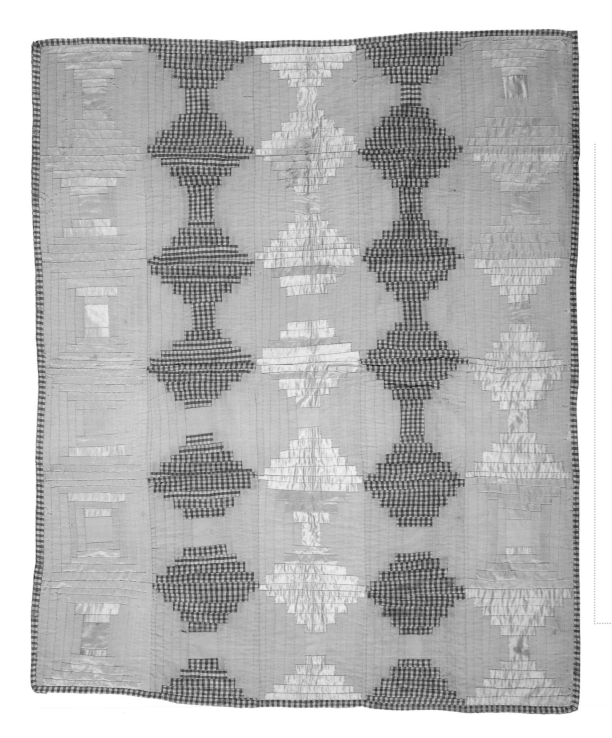

OPPOSITE: Detail of Friendship Album quilt. Block shows machine quilting, which was unusual for that period. Signature, done with pen and ink, reads Mrs. George N. Clarke, Menosha, Wis. Aug. 4, 1881.
Courtesy Ed and Dee King

LEFT: Log Cabin Courthouse Steps, unknown actress, Tombstone, Arizona, 1883; pieced silk and wool challis, 35" x 41."
Collection of Arizona Historical Society, Southern Arizona Division Museum

Howell had spent most of her life in the West. Faced with devastating losses of loved ones, family homes, and the very cause for which they fought the Howells, like many Southerners, made a new start in the West. They had lived briefly in Montana, Utah, and Nevada, and were on their way to Texas in 1879 when they encountered John Slaughter in New Mexico. Over the objections of her mother, Viola, age eighteen, married the thirty-seven-year-old Slaughter. Resigned to the match, her parents combined their small herd with the Slaughter cattle and continued on to Arizona with the newlyweds.

Settling along the San Pedro River, Viola Slaughter's first home as a bride was made of tree branches set in the ground and caulked with mud; it had a dirt floor. Slaughter began a wholesale and retail meat market, bringing in more cattle from Texas until his herd numbered more than two thousand. Since Viola felt her proper place was with her husband, she often accompanied John on cattle drives and other trips, despite the fact that she was "dreadfully afraid of the Indians" and was "forever making Indians and outlaws out of...cacti on the desert."

In 1884, the Slaughters bought the San Bernardino Ranch along the Mexican border. Part of an old Mexican land grant, the 65,000 acre spread continued into Mexico; Viola described her first view of it: "The valley stretched far out before us down into Mexico, rimmed and bounded by mountains all around... thrill of knowing it was all ours, [that] our future lay within it. It was beautiful."

The vast San Bernardino had been deserted for more than fifty years because of Apache raids. In 1886, when General Crook held his historic meeting with Geronimo at Cañon de los Embudos on the Slaughter property, Viola asked to witness the event, but the officer in charge "would allow no one to accompany him or his men."

The family also maintained a home in Tombstone so that John's two children, loved by Viola as her own, could attend school. When low cattle prices were followed by a drought,

ABOVE: Cora Viola Howell Slaughter, age 18, in her wedding dress, 1879. Her jewelry was a wedding gift from her husband John Slaughter.
Courtesy Arizona Historical Society Library

LEFT: Feather Plumes with Coxcombs quilt made by Cora Viola Howell Slaughter (1860–1941) and Edith Stowe (?–1938), Slaughter Ranch, Cochise County, Arizona, c. 1890; appliquéd cotton, 70" x 75."
Collection of Arizona Historical Society, Southern Arizona Division Museum

OPPOSITE: Viola Slaughter and Apache May, 1896. The year-old girl was found by John Slaughter in a raided Apache camp. She was raised on the Slaughter ranch until her death in an accident four years later.
Courtesy Arizona Historical Society Library

Viola felt they should give up the town home and live only on the ranch. Although her husband thought otherwise, Viola insisted "We'll all go out there and put our shoulders to the wheel. We can't give up now and I can help...just you give me a plain house with wide board floors, muslin ceilings, and board finishes around the adobes. That's all I want. But I'm coming out."

They moved to the ranch, sixty-five miles away, in 1892, and began building a large home. It was soon filled with various foster children, including an Apache child found by John in a raided camp in May of 1896.

As the ranch prospered, the Slaughters acquired fine furniture, an organ, a sewing machine, as well as a multi-paned mail-order window for the living room. The ranch was open to everyone traveling through the area. The Slaughters had several servants, which allowed Viola a lifestyle unlike most ranch wives. She could sleep late in the mornings and dress for dinner; she certainly had ample time for needlework, and created this unusual appliqué quilt, its striking design resembling feather plumes. The green plumes are arranged on a white background, with smaller red and gold stylized feathers in between. It is likely that her friend, Edith Stowe, helped with the quilt.

The practical crazy quilts, or "soogans," made by Alice

Gillette Haught utilized any bits of available fabric. The soogans tell of her hard life as a pioneer in one of Arizona's most rugged areas, the Mogollon Rim country north of Payson. Born in Iowa in 1866, when Alice was ten years old, her family took up land in Indian Territory, which became Oklahoma. After her mother's death, as the oldest daughter, Alice helped her father raise the younger children.

Her responsibilities fulfilled in 1886, Alice joined her sister and brother-in-law on a wagon train to New Mexico. Alice was twenty, bordering on being an old maid, and her father had encouraged her to marry forty-year-old, "Mr. Moon" who was also on the wagon train. Alice promised she would "study on it," which greatly encouraged Mr. Moon. Along the way Pete Haught joined the travelers. Pete later said "When I laid eyes on that little red-haired thing with the pansy eyes, I decided that if she was going to waste her life, it might just as well be with me." Much to the distress of Mr. Moon, Pete and Alice were married in White Oaks, New Mexico, on June 22, 1886. After spending several years in White Oaks helping Alice's brother-in-law establish a sawmill, they traveled on to the rim country of Arizona Territory, Pete's original destination, to join his family in a sawmill business.

Recalling the first time she looked out over the Mogollon

ABOVE: Pete and Alice Gillette Haught with 3 sons, c. 1910, Payson, Arizona.
Courtesy Pat Cline

LEFT: Detail of sunflower in center of "soogan." Soogan quilt made by Alice Amelia Gillette Haught (1864–1962), Payson, Arizona, C. 1907; pieces of velvet, cotton, corduroy, wool, and others, pieced and appliquéd, wool batting, 65" x 82."
Courtesy Pat Cline

Rim, Alice said pine trees seemed to grow out of craggy rock and that she looked out at row upon row of purple mountains. Below, almost straight down, stretched a pine-studded valley. As the wagon started down the road that had been carved out of the sheer grey granite rocks, "It looked just like the end of the world," she said.

Alice and Pete homesteaded in Star Valley, just below the rim. To keep her family warm through the cold winter nights, Alice made camp quilts, or as she called them, soogans. They were truly "crazy quilts." Alice's granddaughter, Pat Cline, fondly recalls her grandmother and her soogans. "I know that grandmother wasn't too particular about what she put on those quilts, if (one of them) got a hole in it she patched it with something, with whatever. And she was real long on velvet, or anything fancy." The soogans reflect that whimsy and longing for "anything fancy." In addition to velvet patches, they contain bits of lace trim and even the tags from ready-made clothes. "If you want to know the truth, those quilts are the most colorful thing I can ever remember in her life," her granddaughter said.

TAMING THE FRONTIER

With the Indian Wars ended, a new sense of security allowed many communities to grow and to develop some of the refinements of Eastern society. Women were often the leaders in starting schools, building churches, and organizing libraries. At an 1870 meeting, when the cactus was being cleared to build the town of Phoenix, one woman spoke up and demanded, "First public house you men build has got to be a school. We don't want our children to be brought up like little hellions.

ABOVE: *Mary Smith c. 1900.*
Courtesy Mrs. John W. Lawler

LEFT: *Star of Bethlehem quilt made by Mary Josephine Smith Lawler (1873–1958), Prescott, Arizona, c. 1930; machine-pieced cotton, 77" x 90."*
Courtesy Mrs. John W. Lawler

OPPOSITE: *Mary Lawler driving wagon near Hillside Mine. The trip from the mine to Hillside Station took 11 hours by wagon or 8 hours by buggy.*
Courtesy Mrs. John W. Lawler

Get a teacher with some sense and pay him a fair wage."

The desire for culture was also alive and well in the northern part of the territory. In 1895, a group of women who called themselves the "Monday Club," took books from their own homes and started the first library in Prescott, a clear sign that this rowdy mining town was settling down.

Mary Smith came to Prescott in 1894 to work at the Burke Hotel. She had first come to Arizona as a "Harvey Girl," one of many young women who came West to work at the chain of tourist hotels and restaurants established by Fred Harvey in cooperation with the Santa Fe Railroad. Through her job, Mary met many interesting travelers, including the Corticelli family, owners of a large silk factory in the East.

After a fire destroyed much of downtown Prescott, including the Burke Hotel, in 1900, Mary returned to help the owner rebuild. As head housekeeper at the new St. Michael's Hotel, she used her sewing skills to make most of the curtains and bedspreads for the hotel. The St. Michael's became a prominent gathering place in Prescott, and while working at the hotel, Mary met the Lawler brothers. In 1903, she married William Lawler whose brother John had discovered the Hillside mine; after she married, Mary Smith Lawler lived for fourteen years at the Hillside mine.

The mine was located in a rugged, remote place called Boulder Canyon, in the high desert near Bagdad. All supplies had to be packed in, but Mary brought a woman's touch to the mine by growing fresh fruits, vegetables, and even flowers. A 1906 receipt shows that she purchased ten fig trees, twenty blackberry plants, and four rosebushes for the Hillside Mine, a total bill of nine dollars and sixty cents.

At the mine Mary learned to do whatever tasks were needed. If the Chinese cook was sick, she would step in to do the cooking for the crew. She also helped weigh the gold and often drove the wagon to haul supplies to the mine. It was a thirty-two-mile ride by wagon just to pick up the mail, but she was sometimes rewarded with a bundle of silk samples from the Corticellis. To relax in the evenings, Mary would piece quilts from these colorful bits of silk by lamplight. Mary's daughter-in-law, Helen Lawler said, "She was very conscious of having something beautiful, like her quilts. It was a very hard life, but she never thought of it as a hard life, as long as she could do hand work."

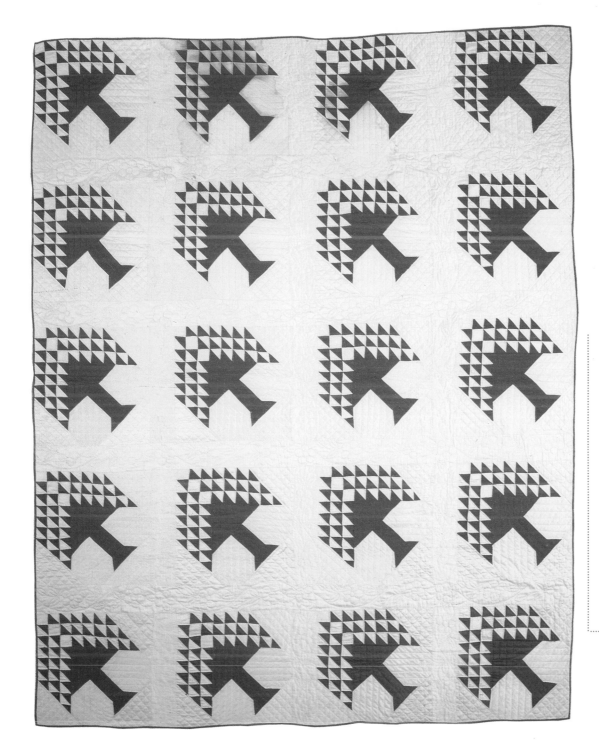

ABOVE: Mary and friends by saguaro cactus near Bagdad, Arizona, 1909.
Courtesy Mrs. John W. Lawler

LEFT: Pine Tree quilt made by Mary Josephine Smith Lawler (1873–1958), Prescott, Arizona, c. 1930; pieced cotton sateen, 75" x 93."
Courtesy Mrs. John W. Lawler

OPPOSITE: Detail, Pine Tree quilt, flowers quilted in sashing.

Later in her life, Mary returned to Prescott to live. Every year she made at least one quilt, which she gave to the Catholic church for a fund-raising raffle. Mary often said that the fourteen years she spent at the Hillside mine were the happiest of her life.

Like Mary Lawler, many pioneers have fond memories of their early days. They had a sense that they were building a new life in a new land. No where was that more true than in the Salt River Valley at the turn of the century. The desert of central Arizona was not settled by Anglo-Americans until the late 1860s. It was the flowing Salt River that attracted them, but it was also the curse of their existence. Years of drought alternated with years of floods. The water of the Salt made life and farming possible in the desert, and then flood waters of the desert river washed away man's hard-built canals, fields, and roads. By 1900, plans were underway to build a dam to control the flow of the mighty Salt River.

In 1908, the engineer in charge of construction of the massive Roosevelt Dam was Louis C. Hill. His brother Edwin, or "Eddie," suffered from tuberculosis, and Louis encouraged him to move to Arizona. Eddie and his bride made the move, and Louis helped him get a job with the U.S. Bureau of Reclamation as the gatekeeper at Granite Reef Dam. Eddie brought his print-ing press and the childhood quilt he had made himself with him to Arizona Territory.

At a time when self-sufficency sometimes meant survival, it was not unusual for boys to be taught rudimentary sewing skills. Frances Bliss Hill believed that boys as well as girls should master the art of sewing, and so each child was given his, or her, choice of a major sewing project to complete. Eddie chose to make a quilt, a simple double-four-patch with red-and-white pinstripe sashing between the blocks. He completed the patchwork in 1876, when he was ten. It is believed that he also quilted it himself. The quilt is signed "Eddie B. Hill" on the inside border.

This quilt reflects Eddie's early talent for careful, precise work, which developed into a passion for printing. In 1882, at the age of sixteen, Eddie acquired his first printing press; later, he worked many years as a printer in Detroit for the *Michigan Christian Herald.* Then, in 1901, Eddie developed tuberculosis and spent the next seven years living in the Michigan woods, an existence much like that of the poet Henry David Thoreau whom he so admired.

After their move to Arizona, the Hills lived for ten years at remote Granite Reef Dam. The closest town was Mesa, fifteen miles to the southwest, reached only by a rough road through a

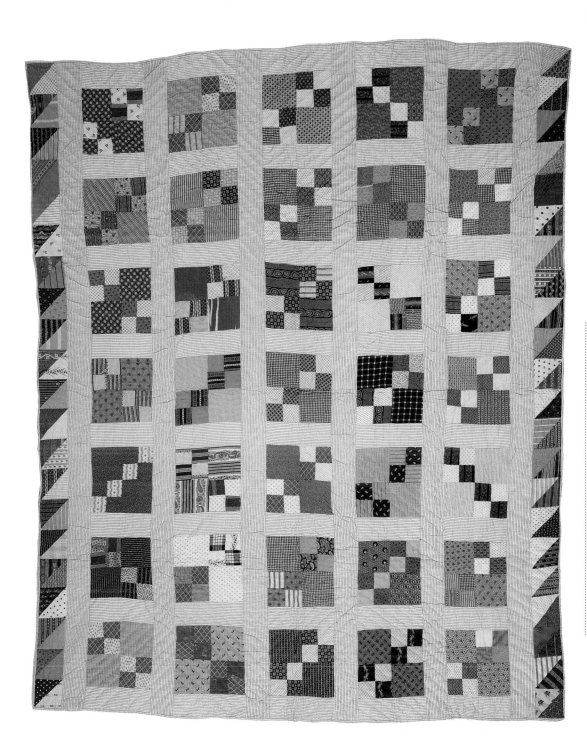

ABOVE: Edwin Bliss Hill, 1901, Michigan.
Courtesy Arizona State University, Hayden Library
Special Collection

LEFT: Double Four-Patch quilt made by
Edwin Bliss Hill (1866–1949), Michigan,
1876; pieced cotton, 67" x 82."
Collection of Tempe Historical Society

OVERLEAF: Former President Theodore
"Teddy" Roosevelt at the dedication of
Roosevelt Dam, March 18, 1911.
Courtesy Salt River Project

pass in the Usery Mountains that took three hours by wagon.

Over his lifetime, Eddie wrote and printed numerous articles, stories, and books about life in the West. His "printer's  mark" was a tiny cowboy hat. During the time the Hill family lived at Granite Reef Dam, Roosevelt Dam was completed, first of a series of man-made dams designed to harness the Salt River and provide a reliable water supply for the desert town of Phoenix.

On March 18, 1911, former President Teddy Roosevelt came to the Salt River Canyon to dedicate the dam that bears his name. The completion of Roosevelt Dam opened many opportunities in the Salt River Valley, and in 1912, when Arizona became the nation's forty-eighth state, a new era was begun. Arizona's statehood marked a new period of growth and prosperity. Those coming to settle here were no longer pioneers in a frontier territory, but residents of our nation's youngest state.

The Woolf family was one of those attracted by the promise of fertile land, plentiful water, and abundant sunshine. Ruth Woolf Jordan was only ten years old in 1912 when her family made the move to Tempe. Her uncle had written to his

family in Arkansas about the building of Roosevelt Dam, the growth of Tempe Normal School, and the prosperity that was coming to the area. Her father came ahead, and Ruth remembers traveling by train with her mother and the rest of the children. In August, they arrived in Maricopa, where they left the train and went by wagon to Tempe. "We thought we'd burn up. We stayed overnight there, sleeping outside. My mother, a proper Southern lady, was horrified. She was sure we would be murdered in our beds," Ruth recalled.

The Woolfs brought many treasured family quilts with them to Arizona; the quilts had been made by Ruth's grandmother and had always been "company quilts." The family rented a home in Tempe, not far from the Salt River. One day while they were at church, their home caught fire, and nearly all of the family's possessions were destroyed. When Ruth's mother Fannie opened the charred wardrobe that held the family bedding, however, she found that the tightly packed quilts still had some undamaged sections in the middle. So Fannie Woolf carefully cut out the good parts, and from the family heirlooms, lovingly created a very unusual quilt. The savaged quilt combines a red-and-white Drunkard's Path quilt with a red-green-and-white Tulip appliqué quilt.

The ability to "make-do" in the worst of circumstances

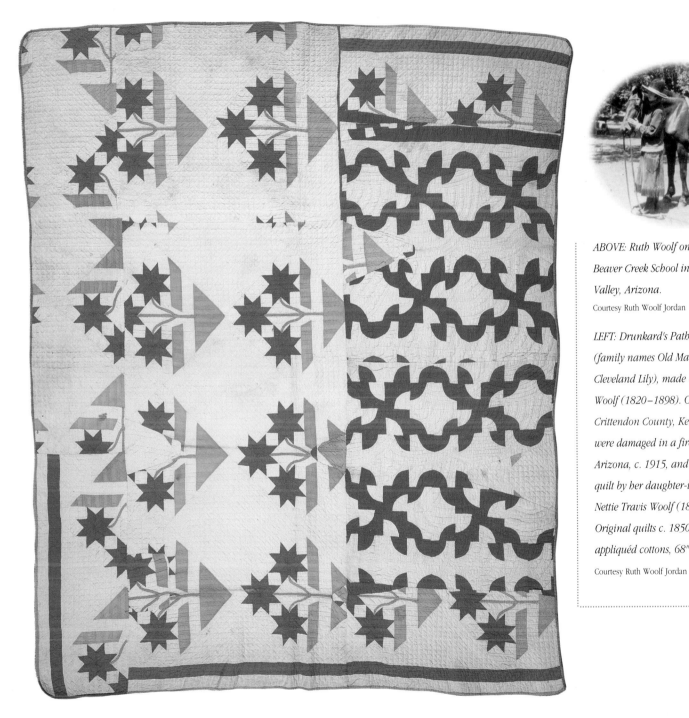

ABOVE: Ruth Woolf on her horse riding to Beaver Creek School in the 1920s, Verde Valley, Arizona.
Courtesy Ruth Woolf Jordan

LEFT: Drunkard's Path/Carolina Lily quilt (family names Old Maid Puzzle / Cleveland Lily), made by Martha Baker Woolf (1820–1898). Originally made in Crittendon County, Kentucky, the quilts were damaged in a fire in Tempe, Arizona, c. 1915, and combined into one quilt by her daughter-in-law, Fannie Nettie Travis Woolf (1897–1936). Original quilts c. 1850–1870, pieced and appliquéd cottons, 68" x 81."
Courtesy Ruth Woolf Jordan

served Arizona women well. Ruth remembered that lesson when she encountered problems later in her life. She received her teaching certificate from the Tempe Normal School in 1920 and became the teacher at the one-room school on Beaver Creek in Rimrock. While teaching, Ruth met and married Walter Jordan when she was twenty-seven years old, in July 1930. The wedding was held in Tempe, early in the morning to avoid the summer heat. The Jordans were pioneer ranchers in the Verde Valley, and as newlyweds, Ruth and her husband joined Walter's brother George and his wife in beautiful Oak Creek Canyon. With plentiful water from Oak Creek, they established apple and peach orchards and a prosperous fruit business beneath the towering red rocks. The Jordan orchards became a landmark in the tiny town of Sedona, and Ruth Woolf Jordan became friends with the town's namesake, Sedona Schnebly.

Sedona Arabella Miller, born in 1877, was one of twelve children in a prosperous Missouri family. Her unusual name was simply made up by her mother; after naming eleven other children, she may have exhausted all other possibilities.

Sedona married Theodore Carlton Schnebly on her twentieth birthday, over her father's strong objections. Four years later, persuaded by favorable reports from Carl's brother Ellsworth, who had gone West for his health, in 1901, the young couple and their two small children decided to go to Arizona Territory. Sedona's father did everything he could to dissuade them from going to "Indian Territory," including threatening to write them out of his will. When the Schneblys made their move, he made good his threat.

Sedona and Carl Schnebly purchased an eighty-acre farm in the area of Arizona then known as Upper Oak Creek Crossing. Within two years of their arrival, the Schneblys had established a grocery store, a profitable truck farm, and a hotel of sorts. Carl built his family a two-story, eleven-room frame house; they welcomed paying guests into their home, or to pitch tents on their property. When Carl applied for a post office for the community, he submitted the name of Oak Creek Crossing and Schnebly Station. Both were rejected because of their length. Ellsworth Schnebly then suggested they name the new town "Sedona."

Their life was ideal until a freak accident one evening. As Sedona and her children herded the family milk cows, five-year-old Pearl was thrown from her pony, with the reins somehow around her neck. She was dragged and trampled to death

ABOVE: Sedona Schnebly with her son Ellsworth, 2 months, Gorin, Missouri, May 11, 1898.
Courtesy Paula Schnebly Hokanson

LEFT: Bear's Paw quilt made by Sedona Miller Schnebly (1877–1950), Sedona, Arizona, 1934; pieced rayon taffeta, 74" x 89."
Courtesy Patricia Schnebly Ceballos and Paula Schnebly Hokanson

OPPOSITE: Sedona Miller Schnebly and Theodore Carlton Schnebly, about the time of their marriage, February 1897, Gorin, Missouri.
Courtesy Paula Schnebly Hokanson

by the terrified horse as her mother watched helplessly. Sedona cut up her wedding dress to make a shroud for the little girl. After Pearl's death, the grief-stricken Sedona weakened and withdrew from life. On the advice of doctors, the Schneblys returned to Missouri.

Within a few years, they left Missouri and homesteaded in Colorado, where they had three more children. In the early 1930s, after losing their cattle to weather and disease, they returned to Sedona, Arizona, where their original farm had been sold and the house had burned to the ground. Their circumstances much reduced, Carl worked as a farm hand for their former neighbors and Sedona did laundry. Always active in the community, the Schneblys were known in Sedona as Father Carl and Aunt Dona.

Despite her years of tragedy and hard work, or perhaps because of them, Sedona made a number of special quilts for her family. She made a traditional Bear's Paw pattern using rayon taffeta instead of the usual cotton and an unusual color combination of rosy reds; warm, glowing peach; rust; and dusty blue tones. Perhaps the colors were inspired by the sculptured red rocks and blue sky of the land where the quilt was made.

The quilts made and brought to Arizona by pioneers witnessed lawless frontier towns become prosperous communities. They saw rutted, dirt roads become paved, tree-lined streets. They saw wagons and horses replaced by automobiles and airplanes. Arizona pioneers' quilts witnessed history.

These quilts have also witnessed the hard work of daily life. Births, deaths, and marriages, joys and sorrows. The routine of raising children, cooking, and sewing is stitched into the quilts of women who came to Arizona to make a home in a new land.

ABOVE: *Elsworth and Pearl Schnebly, Nov. 6, 1900, Gorin, Missouri. When she was 5, Pearl was killed in a freak accident with a horse in Sedona, Arizona.*
Courtesy Paula Schnebly Hokanson

LEFT: *Carl and Sedona Schnebly, 1943, Sedona, Arizona. The Schneblys celebrated their 50th wedding anniversary on February 24, 1947.*
Courtesy Paula Schnebly Hokanson

Compass and Chain quilt made by Pearl Chambers, Willcox, Arizona, c. 1930; pieced cotton, 65" X 85." (see p. 44.)

Courtesy Verna Chambers

FABRIC OF THEIR LIVES

Daily Life Reflected in Quilts

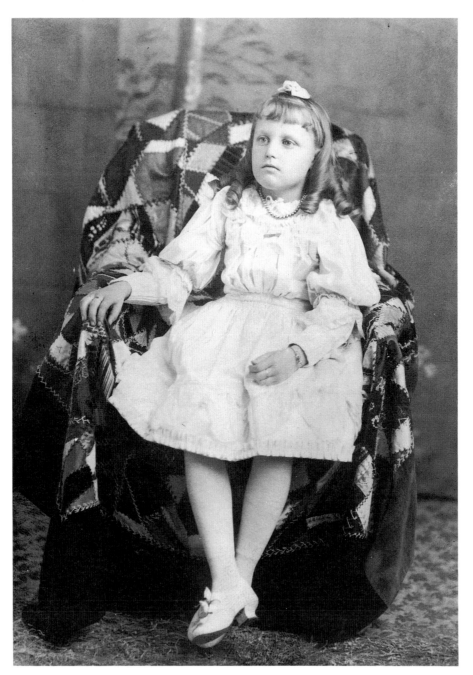

Grace Zeimer Kingman, Arizona Territory.

Courtesy Avery Collection, Arizona Historical Society Library

For generations, sewing was part of a woman's daily life. Like cooking or cleaning, making and mending clothes for a growing family were never-ending tasks. Even though it was time-consuming work, for many women, quiltmaking offered a respite from practical sewing chores. The opportunity to sit quietly while stitching was a rare pleasure in a woman's busy life. Even in a simple scrap quilt, she could enjoy seeing patterns emerge as colorful scraps were cut and stitched.

Making a quilt was also a social occasion. Arizona women usually lived on isolated farms or ranches, and getting together to work on a quilt gave them a chance to join with other women in the family, friends, and neighbors to make the work go faster and to share news of the community. Worries, joys, hopes, fears, marriages, births, and deaths were all discussed over the quilt frame. The quilt they made together warmed the soul as well as the body.

Today, these quilts are threads connecting us to our past, a tangible link to our grandmothers, who whisper to us, if we listen, about their lives—their hardships and their hopes. Their quilts are the fabric of their lives.

STITCHED BY SMALL HANDS

Expected to help supply the family with clothing and bedding, young girls were taught basic sewing skills at an early age. Making a sampler, with cross-stitched alphabets and perhaps a verse or scripture, taught both the basic embroidery skills and the alphabet. There was no better exercise, however, for learning to sew a fine seam than the piecing of squares into patchwork. Girls as young as three learned to ply a needle by joining scraps into a four-patch or nine-patch that could be used as a small quilt for their favorite doll or perhaps as the first block of

the many needed for a bed quilt. They also learned practical lessons about patience and perseverance. Often these childhood practice-blocks traveled many miles and waited many years before fulfilling their destiny to be a quilt.

Lena Chipman came from Colorado with her family to Miami, Arizona, where her father and two brothers worked in the copper mines. She brought with her a Checkerboard quilt she had pieced from clothing scraps in 1899, when she was eight years old. Later, when Lena completed the quilt for her hope chest, the six-inch Checkerboard blocks were set alternately with plain red blocks. She called it her "postage stamp" quilt.

In 1918, Lena moved to Payson to teach school. Over the years she made many quilts. She had a sun porch where she set up her quilting frame, and in the summer she and her mother would quilt while enjoying cool pine breezes.

In 1882, Sarah Ann Bowman Cofer found herself and all her worldly possessions in a covered wagon being pulled by two mules across Arizona Territory. Carefully packed in a trunk in the wagon were the quilt blocks she had painstakingly made as an eight-year-old girl. She must have marvelled at the sudden changes in her life as she rode in the wagon holding her infant son. Only a few

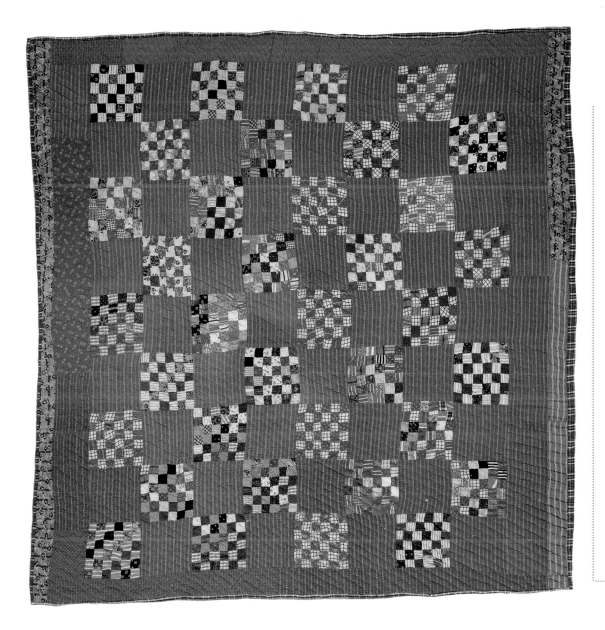

LEFT: Checkerboard quilt made by Lena Chipman Chilson Hampton (1891–1985), Weston, Texas, 1899; pieced cottons, 71" x 72."

Courtesy Bonnie McClanahan

weeks before, in the spring of 1882, she had been living in Stratford, Iowa, surrounded by corn fields and green grass.

Born in 1859, Sarah Ann married Frank Cofer in 1880. They had been married two years and were the parents of a baby son when Frank's father returned from a trip to Arizona Territory. His glowing reports and belief that the area held great promise for young people convinced his sons, Frank and George, to go to Arizona and, if they liked the country, to return for their families. The young wives would not agree; afraid as they were of traveling into "wild Injun country," they would not stay behind. The party traveled by train as far as New Mexico, where the railroad line ended; from there, they traveled by wagon to northwestern Arizona.

The Cofer family established a ranch on the Big Sandy River, south of Wikieup. A trip north to the town of Kingman for provisions took a week: three days of travel in each direction and one day in town. For seventeen years, they lived in a "stick-in-the-mud" house on the ranch. It wasn't until 1899, after the birth of four more children, that a frame house was built under the cottonwood trees. Even then, only the great room, a bedroom, and a bath had wooden floors; the rest of the rooms had dirt floors covered with straw and tightly stretched burlap.

Sarah Ann covered the burlap with her handmade braided rugs. Well-known for her braided rugs made from scraps, she took pride in the fact that they were "flat as a table and without a buckle." She never wasted a scrap of material; old denims were cut up and used with outing flannel to make hardy camp quilts. Even the string used to tie them was saved from flour and sugar sacks.

It wasn't until she moved to Kingman in the 1920s that Sarah Ann finally stitched together and quilted the little blocks she had made as a child and brought with her to Arizona.

Betty Mae Cravey Williams was another young girl who completed her ambitious childhood quilt. Betty learned the value of thrift as a child from her grandmother, whose motto was, "Never waste anything and make use of everything." The Cravey family lived in the tiny town of Anita, in the pines and ranchlands of northwestern Arizona, when Betty was

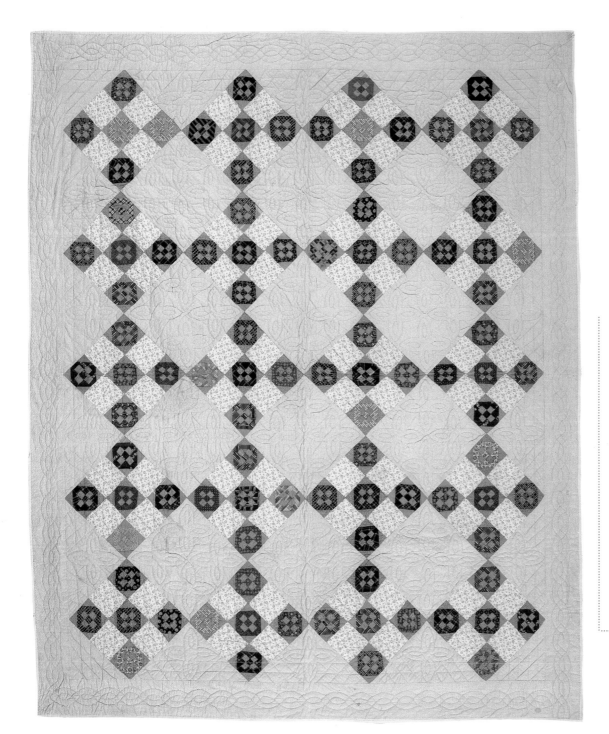

ABOVE: Sarah Bowman Cofer, c. 1880, Stratford, Iowa.
Courtesy Jennielee Cofer Bishop

LEFT: Double Wrench quilt made by Sarah Bowman Cofer (1859–1929). The blocks were made in Iowa in 1867 and set together and quilted in Kingman, Arizona, in 1929; pieced cotton, 68" x 82."
Courtesy Jennielee Cofer Bishop

OPPOSITE: Betty Cravey, age 8, dressed as a cowboy, 1933, Anita, Arizona.
Courtesy Betty Cravey Williams

born in 1925. Her father worked as guide for tourists in the Grand Canyon, hunted mountain lions, and trapped for furs. Considering that a year of trapping might yield as little as five hundred dollars, money was often tight. Fabrics were especially hard to obtain. When she could, Betty's mother sent a dollar to a cousin in Los Angeles who worked in a clothing factory. He then sent remnants that the family used for dresses, curtains, and quilts.

Ten-year-old Betty often watched the Babbitt Ranch cowboys at work. The cowboys carried small muslin bags filled with tobacco used to roll their own cigarettes, and it occurred to her that these discarded Bull Durham tobacco sacks could be stitched together to make a quilt. When they noticed her collecting them, the cowboys began to save the little sacks for Betty.

Over the course of three years, Betty carefully stitched dozens of the small, white tobacco sacks together. On each rectangular block she embroidered a cattle brand in pink, blue, yellow, green, or red. The brands were copied from nearby ranches, found in a book on brands, or the wrapping paper from Porter's Western Store in Phoenix. When her quilt top was complete, she quilted it with a horseshoe pattern around the border.

SOMETHING FROM NOTHING

Pearl Chambers, of Willcox, made the most of small scraps of fabric when she created a warm Brick Wall pattern quilt using

wool pieces from a tailors' sample book. The quilt was made in 1928 by joining the rectanglar pieces of wool from *The Royal Taylors Spring Weights-Season 1926* sample book. Yellow and tan feather stitching over the seams added a decorative touch to this practical quilt, which was tied with green yarn.

Not all Pearl's quilts were as thrifty or practical as her Brick Wall quilt; however, she demonstrated her artistic side in 1937 when she made a dramatic Compass and Chain pattern quilt as a high school graduation present for her son Clell. Using new fabrics in patriotic red, white, and blue, this striking quilt was obviously very special.

Like Pearl Chambers, many prolific quiltmakers made numerous simple quilts for "every day" and relished the opportunity to make a quilt for "company" or for a gift. In these special quilts, a woman could let her creativity shine, creating art from her scrap bag.

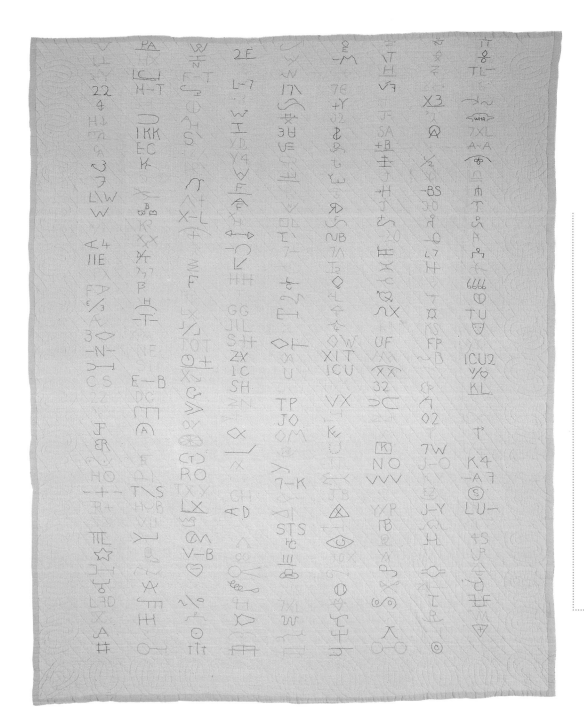

ABOVE: Detail of Arizona Brands quilt shows embroidered brands.

LEFT: Arizona Brands quilt made by Betty Cravey Williams (1925–), Anita, Arizona, 1938; Bull Durham cotton tobacco sacks, 81" x 102."
Courtesy Betty Cravey Williams

OPPOSITE: The Royal Taylor's Spring Weights-Season 1926 sample book. Blanks show where wool samples were removed to make the Brick Wall quilt.
Courtesy Clell and Verna Chambers

ABOVE: *Pearl Norwood and Cornelius "Neal" Chambers, wedding photo, 1906, Ripley, Oklahoma. Pearl and Neal Chambers were married in Texas and moved to Sulphur Springs Valley in south-eastern Arizona in 1909. Neal Chambers was a miner and rancher. Pearl had 5 children and belonged to the Sulphur Springs Homemakers Club, members of which occasionally got together to quilt.*
Courtesy Clell & Verna Chambers

RIGHT: *Brick Wall quilt made by Pearl Chambers (1886–1961), Willcox, Arizona, 1926; pieced wool samples, 54" x 75."*
Courtesy Clell & Verna Chambers

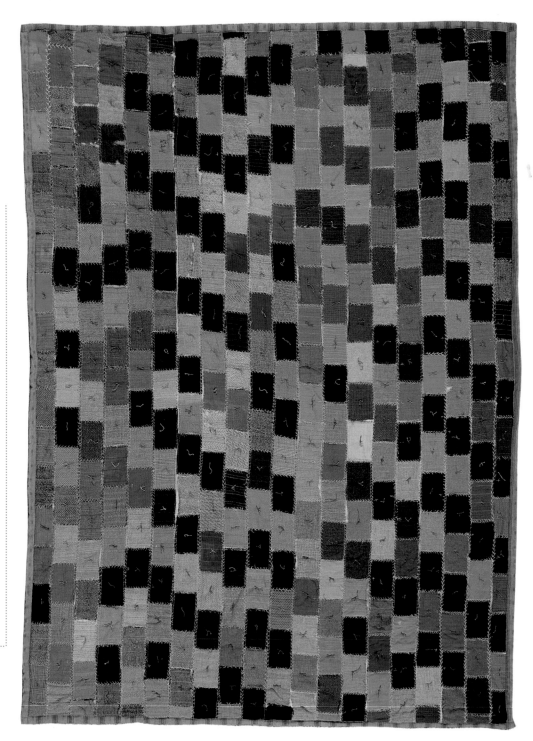

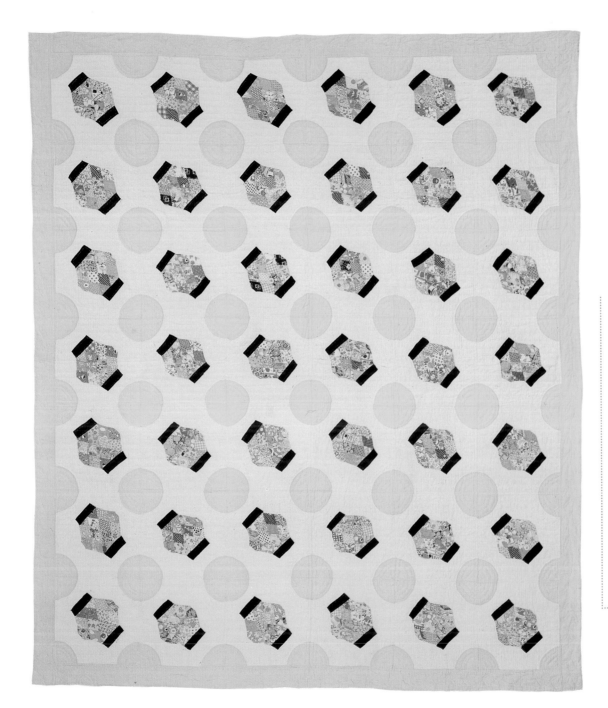

ABOVE: Mary Catherine Ragan Gilson,
c. 1900.
Courtesy Lucy Campbell

LEFT: Chinese Lantern quilt made by
Mary Catherine Ragan Gilson
(1876–1950) Williams, Arizona, c. 1930;
pieced cotton, 72" x 80."
Courtesy Lucy Campbell

Mary Gilson was one such artist. The Gilsons came to Arizona in 1895 and settled in Williams, a small railroad and ranching community in the pines between Flagstaff and the Grand Canyon. There the Gilsons raised three sons and a daughter. John was a blacksmith by trade but became a mechanic when automobiles began to replace horses as transportation. Mary Gilson did washing, ironing, and quilting for people, charging not by the spool but by the quilt. In the 1920s, she charged five dollars to quilt a Grandmother's Flower Garden quilt.

Mary generally kept a quilt frame set up in her living room. Her daughter, Lucy Campbell, remembers that her mother used every spare moment for quilting, usually not for long stretches, but rather a few stitches at a time. Lucy recalls that in addition to quilting, Mary kept busy piecing quilts; "she was always sitting at the machine and running up a Nine Patch."

In winter, snow blanketed the town of Williams. The Gilson family's "everyday" quilts, made for warmth, were simple pieced cottons, made on a newspaper foundation, crazy-quilt style, which were tied, not quilted. Nevertheless, Mary liked to have "something nice to put on the bed for company," so she made special quilts for such occasions.

The family called one of these "company" quilts Japanese Lantern. (The more commonly accepted name for this pattern is Chinese Lantern.) Even for this special quilt, Mary made good use of her scrap bag. Each lantern is pieced from scraps, set off with a black base and top. The quilt is made more dramatic by bright yellow circles between the lanterns, created where yellow corners on the blocks come together. The yellow border is quilted with a pattern of vines and leaves. Mary pieced the Lantern quilt on her Singer treadle sewing machine and quilted it on her custom-made frames, which were extra-high so Mary could quilt comfortably while sitting erect.

Part Cherokee Indian, Ethie Maude Brown Pittman was born in Texas in 1890. In 1930, she and her husband followed their oldest daughter and moved to Florence, Arizona. In Florence the Pittmans farmed cotton, and Maude made many outstanding scrap quilts. Using feed sacks and other scraps, she adapted familar patterns, creating original designs or color combinations. Her Star of Many Points variation also has an unusual double border of pieced triangles.

LEFT: *Star of Many Points quilt made by*
Ethie Maude Brown Pittman,
(1890 – 1982), Florence Arizona, 1936;
pieced cotton feed sacks, 67" x 82."
Courtesy Hazel Wilson

OPPOSITE: *Maude Pittman, c. 1930.*
Courtesy Hazel Wilson

Bessie Freeman Woods was born in Louisana, went to college in Texas, married, and moved to Tucson with her husband in 1908, where she and her family owned and operated the Fairview Dairy until 1960. Despite her many responsiblities at the dairy, Bessie was a prolific quilter. Her daughter, Ruth Woods Bradford, recalls that her mother always had piecework in her hands. "She had what was called a scrap bag, and there was nothing in the scrap bag except new materials; she never made quilts from any material that was used."

In the 1920s and 1930s, more and more women came to have responsibilities outside the home, but quilting continued to play a part in their lives, if not for necessity, then for pleasure and relaxation.

Bessie's favorite pattern was the Star, and she made Ruth a Star quilt when she got married. "The thing I liked about her quilts [was that] so many of her materials were scraps from things that she had made, or I had made, or that I knew someone who had used 'em, so lots of memories are tied up in a family quilt."

Not all memories stitched into a quilt were happy ones. Hazel Maude Smith Cardin Talkington and her husband came to Arizona from Oklahoma in 1932, hired to cook for the Forest Service crews building fire roads in the rugged Mogollon Rim country. They lived in tents at the worker's camp at General Springs, and it was there that Hazel hand-pieced the Glorified Nine Patch quilt using scraps and new pink fabric. She had the top quilted by a woman in Flagstaff and gave it to her daughter-in-law in the 1940s. Piecing the quilt had filled some otherwise empty hours, but Hazel forever equated quilts with poverty.

By contrast, many women who lived hard, simple lives found quiltmaking to be a practical outlet for quiet relaxation and creativity. Mary Eagar Brown was one such woman. Mary was born in 1881 in the Mormon settlement of Springerville, just north of the town of Eagar, which was founded by her father's family. She was only seventeen when her mother died, which left Mary with the bulk of household chores, including the task of making bedding for the family. Married in 1901 to Lorenzo Brown II, a farmer, Mary bore ten children; one, a three-year-old boy, was killed in an accident with a horse.

In 1914, the family moved to Fort Thomas in the Pima Valley, where Lorenzo wintered mules and horses. There he began to realize his dream of owning a ranch when he acquired cattle and purchased land. Times had been hard, but things were beginning to get better for the Brown family when Lorenzo was tragically killed in a car-train accident in 1922.

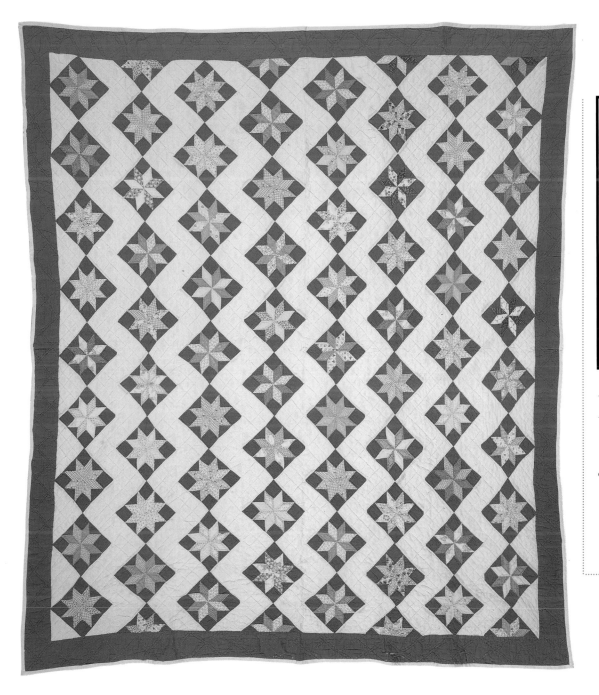

"The thing I liked about her quilts [was that] so many of her materials were scraps from things that she had made, or I had made, or that I knew someone who had used 'em, so lots of memories are tied up in a family quilt."

Ruth Woods Bradford

LEFT: Eight-Pointed Stars quilt made by Bessie Freeman Woods (1878–1967), Tucson, Arizona, c. 1930; pieced cotton blocks set with lightning sashing, 65" x 77."
Courtesy Ruth Woods Bradford

This left Mary with eight children to raise (the oldest daughter had married) and a farm to run. Eventually she was forced to sell some of the land and cattle, but Mary was a hard worker and was determined to support and keep her family together. They raised large gardens and their own meat, and as soon as the boys were old enough they went to work for the railroad and brought their earnings home to their mother.

Mary was a busy woman. In addition to caring for her large family, she gave time to the Mormon Church as Relief Society president. Quilting was what she did to relax; when she sat down, she would pick up her piecing. When she was ready to quilt, she gathered her four daughters and they shared pleasant times quilting together. Busy with gardens in the spring and fall months, Mary and her daughters did most of their quilting in the winter and summer. One daughter's husband owned a dairy farm and gave Mary empty feed sacks; once they were bleached, she used them for pillowcases, dish towels, and even underwear, as well as quilt backings. Another daughter and son-in-law owned a dry goods store, where Mary obtained fabric to sew her children's clothes. The scraps from these clothes gave Mary ample material for her quiltmaking, and cotton raised in the Pima Valley provided the batting.

FIGURATIVE APPLIQUÉ

Through the centuries, quilt patterns were passed from one woman to another. At times, particular quilt styles have enjoyed special popularity. In the 1930s, when quiltmaking enjoyed renewed popularity, magazines and newspapers printed patterns and certain styles spread quickly across the country. From Arizona to New England, quilts depicting a country girl, known as Sunbonnet Sue, were a favorite.

The fact that feedsacks provided much of the fabric for quilts made by Mary Brown didn't prevent her from creating the latest Sunbonnet Sue designs. Sue's dresses and bonnets were made from printed feed sacks embellished with embroidery, and the quilt was backed with bleached feed sack material. The one-inch pieced sashing of the Mary's Sunbonnet Sue quilt made use of a multitude of tiny scraps, reflecting many hours of painstaking hand-piecing.

Appliquéd "Mammy" figures reflect the quiltmaker's sense of humor and her Southern roots. Made in the style of the popular Sunbonnet Sue, this variation depicts the figure as an "Aunt Jemima"–style black woman with a turban. (Similar quilts have been found in Texas and Mississippi.)

ABOVE: Hazel Smith Cardin Talkington, c. 1940.

Courtesy Karen Alexa Cardin Hopkins

LEFT: Glorified Nine Patch made by Hazel Smith Cardin Talkington (1903–1987) General Springs, Arizona, c. 1935; pieced cotton, 61" x 73."

Courtesy Karen Alexa Cardin Hopkins

Sunbonnet Sue quilt made by Mary Eagar
Brown (1881–1969), Fort Thomas, Arizona,
c. 1930; pieced cotton, 71" x 84."

Courtesy Jennie H. Brown

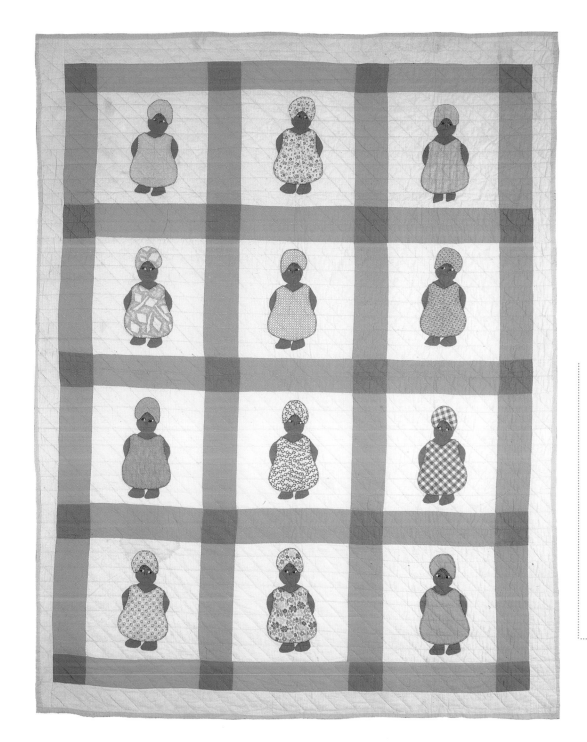

ABOVE: *Veda Godard Hollowwa with daughter Hazel.*
Courtesy Connie Godard Phillips

LEFT: *Mammy quilt made by Veda Buck Godard Hollowwa (1883–1970) Camp Verde, c. 1935; pieced cotton, 69" x 88."*
Courtesy Connie Godard Phillips

Veda Buck Godard Hollowwa made this Mammy Quilt in the early 1930s using scraps from clothes and flour and sugar sacks for the figures' dresses and turbans. She gave each figure a distinct personality and expression by embroidering eyes that look in different directions (even cross-eyed). Black buttonhole stitch embroidery outlines each figure, some of which were stitched by machine and others, by hand.

Born in Arkansas in 1883, Veda Buck was a new bride when she came to Arizona in 1900. She settled with her husband, Lou Godard, on a ranch near Camp Verde. However, the cream, butter, and eggs produced were not enough to support the growing family and a year was spent working at a nearby dairy for money to pay off the ranch.

Sixteen years later, Lou's death left Veda a widow with three children. The ranch was sold for taxes, and she was desperate for a way to support her family. She moved to Phoenix and earned money by doing laundry for others, including the Hollowwa family. After Mrs. Hollowwa's death, Veda married her employer, Isaac Hollowwa, in 1929.

Later, Veda's grown children bought back the Camp Verde ranch for their mother, and Isaac and Veda moved there in 1934. Ranch life was hard, especially without plumbing or electricity; for example, the well was a hundred feet from the

house, and the first bucket drawn usually had frogs or snakes in it and had to be thrown out. It was during this time that Veda made the Mammy quilt.

In addition to Sunbonnet Sue, other simple appliquéd objects were popular with quiltmakers in the thirties. An appliquéd Clipper Ship quilt, made by Ida Belle Casner See during this period (probably from a kit), includes black-embroidered details on the ship's sails and ocean waves.

Ida Belle was one of eleven children born to Riley and Rebecca Casner. In the early 1870s, Riley Casner left Oregon with his first wife and their four children in a wagon train bound for California. His wife and two children died on the trip; after arriving in California, he met and married Rebecca Jane Frezell. The Casners moved to Arizona in 1875 and settled in the Verde Valley.

They homesteaded on Beaver Creek, living in a log cabin for many years. The family planted a large orchard, raised vegetables, and kept cattle, chickens, and goats. The children,

LEFT: Clipper Ship quilt made by Ida Belle Casner See (1890–1984), Camp Verde, 1935; appliquéd cotton, 81" x 100."
Courtesy Jo See and Verde Historical Society

OPPOSITE: Rebecca Casner and 7 daughters (Ida is third from right), Camp Verde, 1926.
Courtesy Jo See and Verde Historical Society

including Ida Belle, born in 1890, were expected to help with the work, and quilting was a routine domestic chore. At thirteen, Ida Belle assumed the responsibility of cooking for the family. When Ida Belle was nineteen, she married Henry (Hank) See, a cattleman twice her age, and they became the parents of four sons. In 1935, Ida pieced a Clipper Ship quilt as a wedding gift for one of her sons, using the skills she had learned as a girl.

The Great Depression gave a new respectabilty to the patchwork quilt and the practice of making something out of nothing. The craft's popularity surged and even nonquilters gave it a try; since most women made the bulk of the family clothing, it was simply a matter of redirecting their sewing skills. One of those who experimented was Lucille Marie Bitting Thornburg, who was persuaded by a bulging scrap bag and a newspaper pattern to make a Fan quilt.

Lucille met and married her husband Martin Lynn Thornburg in her native Indiana. In 1924, they moved to Tucson, close to the University of Arizona, where Martin taught mechanical engineering and eventually became head of the the Department of Engineering. In 1933, when Lucille's seventy-year-old mother, Leila Ada Bitting, moved to Tucson to live with her daughter's family, they decided they would make two quilts, one for each of Lucille's children, Dale and Marilyn.

Lucille had seen a pattern in the newspaper for a Fan quilt. Her husband drafted the pattern and figured the amount of fabric needed. After purchasing material for the border and backing, Lucille and Leila machine-pieced scraps into fan blocks for two identical twin-bed-size quilts. Daughter Marilyn remembers that "all other activities halted" while the blocks were laid out on the dining room and living room. After two or three months of work, the tops were finished and taken to the Ladies Sewing Circle of the First Methodist Church to be quilted.

When completed, the quilts were wrapped and labeled with the children's names, then carefully stored away. In 1973, after Lucille's death, the family discovered the quilts she had so carefully kept.

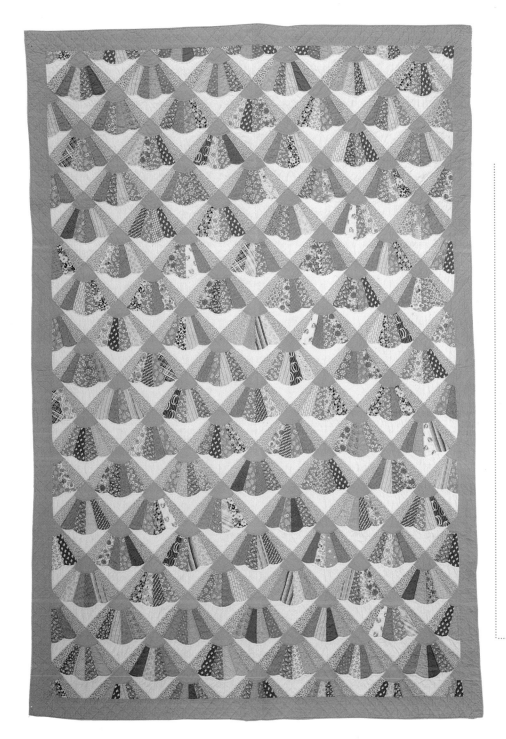

LEFT: *Fan quilt made by Leila Bitting (1864–1943) and Lucille Bitting Thornburg (1892–1973), Tucson, Arizona, 1937; pieced cotton, 68" x 100."*
Courtesy Marilyn A. Thornburg Workman

OPPOSITE: *Thornburg Family (left to right: Lucille, Dale, Leila, Marilyn, and Lynn), Tucson, Arizona, c. 1930.*

REWARDING THE SPIRIT

In Casa Grande, Sarah Orpha Deakins Killingsworth, or Orphie, as she was called, obviously looked beyond the popular patterns of the day for her quilt designs. A talented and prolific quilter, she combined a nineteenth-century quilt pattern, New York Beauty, with 1930s fabrics and colors, creating an interesting juxtaposition of styles.

Orphie Deakins married William Killingsworth in 1883, and the couple spent the early years of their marriage in Georgia, where they farmed and ran a sawmill. By 1914, Orphie was suffering severely from asthma and the dry climate of the Southwest was recommended as a cure.

They settled in Casa Grande, where Orphie kept her quilting frames up and in use almost year-round on a large screened porch. She made many quilts for herself and family, and she also quilted for others, charging "by the spool." At one dollar per spool, the charge for quilting a large bed quilt was usually around eight dollars. Quilt batting was readily available; after World War I, Casa Grande was a thriving cotton farming region, and friends brought Orphie sacks of cotton bolls direct from the fields, which she then carded and made her own batts.

Before she died in 1937, Orphie completed a quilt for each of her six grandchildren, all of whom lived near her in Casa Grande. She pinned a name to each and stored them in a trunk. However, after her death, all of her things, including the quilts, were taken by other family members to Texas. A granddaughter saw her New York Beauty quilt five years later when an uncle came to visit. She offered to buy her uncle a new wool blanket in exchange for the quilt. He agreed, and so one quilt returned to Arizona.

Matching the many points required to make a Mariner's Compass is a challenge to the most skilled quilter, and Alice Jordan Gary chose to include not just one, but twelve, Mariner's Compasses in her skillfully made, red-and-white quilt— just one example of many beautiful quilts she made during her life.

Although married to a Verde Valley rancher, Alice was not a "typical" ranch wife. Born in 1896 in Clarkdale, Alice Jordan married Bill Gray in 1920. On their properous Cottonwood ranch, the Grays raised cattle and horses. Bill often traded his horses on Indian reservations for Indian baskets. Alice Gray had no children and spent a great deal of

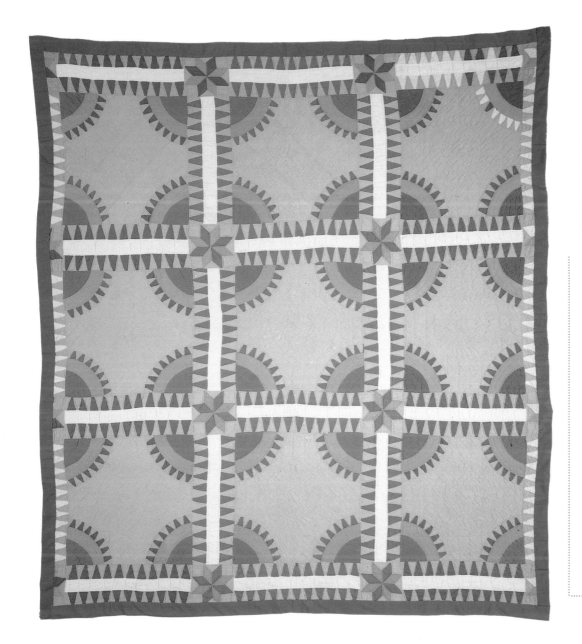

*ABOVE: William and Orpha
Killingsworth and 3 of their children
(left to right, Dexter, Ethel, and
Charlie) in Georgia in 1890, before
coming to Arizona.*
Courtesy Zelpha Killingsworth Watkins

*LEFT: New York Beauty quilt made by
Sarah Orpha Deakins Killingsworth,
(1864–1938), Casa Grande, Arizona,
1933; pieced cotton, 76" x 84."*
Courtesy Zelpha Killingsworth Watkins

*OPPOSITE: Detail of Mariner's
Compass block shows clamshell quilting
in red sashing and flowers and leaves
quilted in white space around compass.*
Courtesy Elnora Jordan

time doing embroidery, decorating pillowcases and other household items. She reportedly did hand appliqué by the hour and also machine-pieced quilts for various family members. Alice preferred needlework to "outside work" and made time for herself by not keeping gardens or even flower beds.

WEDDING BLESSINGS

One of the most popular patterns of the 1930s was the Double Wedding Ring. The many curved pieces challenged a quilter's piecing skill and made good use of scraps. As the name suggests, it was usually stitched for a hope chest or as a wedding gift. Although "bridal white" was most often used for the background, Ity Smith chose red for her Double Wedding Ring quilt made in Globe, Arizona, in the 1930s.

Ity and her daughter Ima sewed all their own clothes. Many of the fabrics used in the Red Double Wedding Ring quilt were scraps of those dresses, but the dramatic red background was probably new fabric purchased especially for this quilt. The quilt was quilted at a Baptist church bee; Ity quilted regularly with her church group and, during World War II, helped make quilts for the Red Cross.

Quilting bees were as much a social gathering as a work session, especially for those women who made quilts for their own use rather than for their church or community. Living proof of the axiom "Many hands make light work," quilting bees could produce a finished quilt in a matter of hours instead of the weeks needed by a solitary quilter.

Pieced from dress scraps by Edith Parme Griswold-Carson in Douglas, Arizona, in the early 1920s, this white Double Wedding Ring quilt was quilted by Mrs. Carson and a group of friends who met in each other's homes once a month.

Mrs. Carson's daughter Grace remembers the times when the group met at her mother's house as very special. The women quilted all afternoon, and sandwiches and coffee were served; Grace, then about nine years old, helped serve the ladies and loved being allowed to turn the handle on the treasured copper coffee urn with a burner underneath. Grace was also encouraged to quilt and had her own corner on which to work.

Like many families, the Carsons came to Arizona for its healthful climate and made it their home for the rest of their lives. James Frederick and Edith Carson arrived in Douglas in spring of 1912, on a day Edith remembered as "horrible, dusty and dirty." Newly married, the Carsons were on their way to California from Pennsylvania in search of a better climate that would possibly help James' tuberculosis.

ABOVE: Alice Ivey Jordan, Cottonwood, Arizona, c. 1915.

Courtesy Elnora Jordan

LEFT: Mariner's Compass quilt by Alice Ivey Jordan Gray (1896 – 1979), Cottonwood, Arizona, c. 1935; pieced cotton, 64" x 85."

Courtesy Elnora Jordan

ABOVE: *Ity Eugene James Smith, Globe, Arizona, c. 1930s. Ity James was born in 1869 in Marian, Georgia. When she was 16, her family moved to Texas, where she married Joseph Smith. They had 5 children, and in 1927 moved to Globe Arizona, near their daughter, Ima.*
Courtesy Elinor Johnson

RIGHT: *Red Double Wedding Ring quilt made by Ity Eugene James Smith (1869–1965) Globe, Arizona, c. 1930; pieced cotton, 65" x 79."*
Courtesy Elinor Johnson & Eugene Cunningham

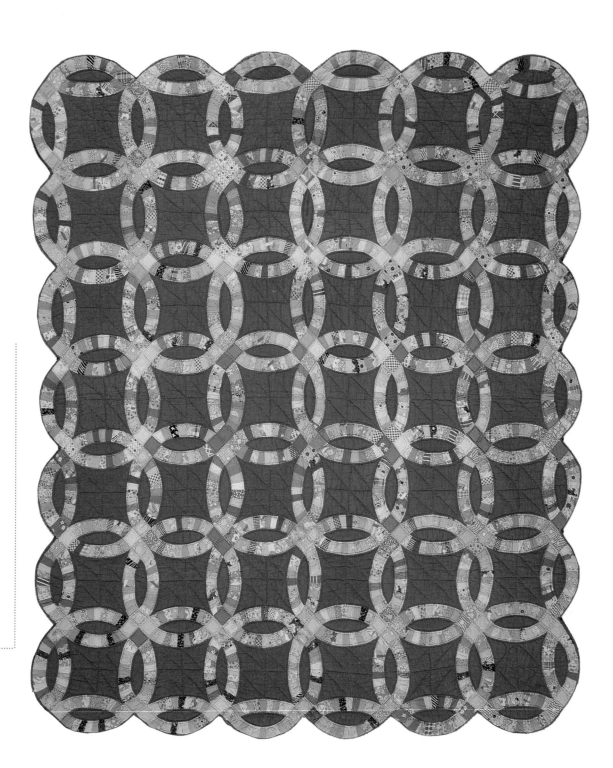

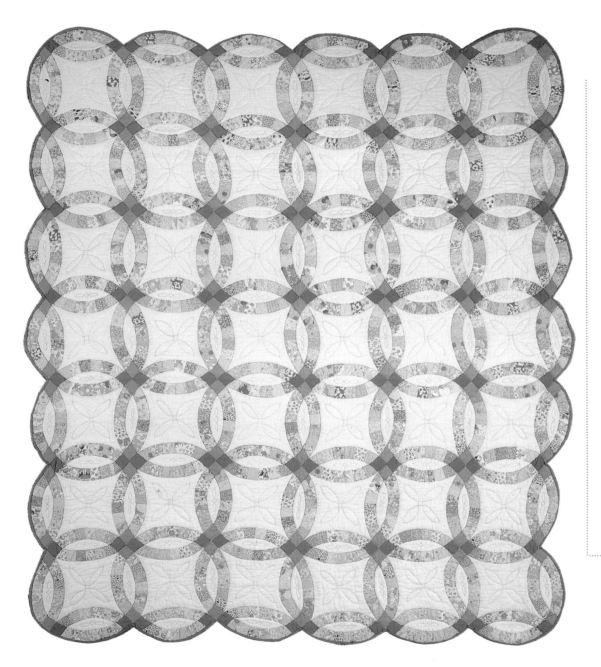

Double Wedding Ring quilt made by Edith Griswold Carson (1888–1973), Douglas, Arizona, c. 1930; pieced cotton, 74" x 79."
Courtesy Mrs. Edith G. Carson

As the train passed from New Mexico into Arizona, James was impressed by the mountains, and the decision was made to settle in Douglas.

This appliquéd Mariner's Compass quilt, made from a rayon-like fabric with a herringbone weave, is not typical of the quilts made by Elsie Vilate Owens DeWitt Flake. Most of her quilts were made for warmth from old coats or pants, with flour sacks as the backing.

Elsie Flake was born in Woodruff, Arizona Territory, in 1882, and grew up knowing hard work very early in life, as her mother was an invalid. Well-educated for a woman of that era, Elsie attended Gila Academy in Thatcher before her marriage at eighteen to Willie DeWitt, a farmer. The oldest of their three children, a son, died after hitting his head against a saddle while watering some horses. A few years later, Elsie's husband died of typhoid fever.

In 1914, Elsie married Joel White Flake, a widower with four children. A cowboy and rancher, Joel Flake moved his family to Snowflake Ranch, near the town of Snowflake.

Laundry was an enormous task for the family, which eventually included thirteen children. A daughter remembers helping make the soap, cooking animal fat and lye until it was the right consistency. It was this homemade soap that Elsie used to clean the wool for her quilts; after scrubbing the raw wool on a washboard, she carded it.

With six unmarried sons out of school, Elsie offered her Mariner's Compass quilt to the first one wed. The fifth son, Clark Owen Flake, was the lucky young man who received the quilt for his wedding in 1936. With its feather and flower designs quilted with small, even stitches, it has always been known by the family as simply "Mama's Quilt."

Over the years, many quilts became a scrapbook of the patchwork memories of daily life: the smile of an infant, the excitement of a new bride setting up a household of her own, or simply a warm bed on a cold night. Other quilts from their inception are a record of history. Friendships, community events, even political campaigns and wars have been recorded by women in their quilts.

ABOVE: Elsie and Joel Flake at Flake ranch near Snowflake, Arizona, c. 1940.
Courtesy Eva Winmill

LEFT: Mariner's Compass quilt made by Elsie Vilate Owens DeWitt Flake (1882–1953), Snowflake, Arizona, c. 1935; appliquéd shiny rayon, 70" x 78."
Courtesy Eva Winmill

Detail of Crazy quilt with fan and embroidered Spanish house with "red tile roof," also border with chenille embroidery flowers.

Collection of Arizona Historical Society, Southern Arizona Division Museum

CHRONICLES IN CLOTH

Quilts as Family and Community Records

Whitmer family, Angus, Jennie, and their 13 children at family gathering, Alpine, Arizona, c. late 1920s.

Courtesy Jennie Campbell

Women have always made "special" quilts to commemorate and celebrate notable personal events. While newspapers and history books recorded elections, wars, bank robberies, and murders, women stitched quilts to record marriages, births, friendships, and community milestones. When we read these special chronicles in cloth, we discover the history of individuals, families, and communities written with thread.

Quilts intended to serve as warm bedcovers were frequently "used up and worn out," but quilts made for special events were spared daily use. They were treasured, gently cared for, and lovingly passed from one generation to the next. Many such quilts are more than a hundred years old and still in excellent condition.

While women in territorial Arizona were geographically far-removed from fashions of the East, they kept in touch with the lastest styles. In the late 1800s, when it became fashionable to use elegant fabrics and fancy embroidery to make what were called "Crazy quilts," Arizona women, too, used their time and talents to create beautiful quilts that could compete with those of their Eastern sisters. Many incorporated dated ribbons and were often embellished with embroidered phrases, names, places, and initials. Flowers, birds, and butterflies were also popular embroidery motifs. The women of Arizona Territory frequently added their own very distinctive motifs.

EMBROIDERED HISTORY

While many quilts graphically record events, places, dates, and even significant aspects of daily life, the maker frequently

neglected to record her own identity, as if to say that she, as historian, was not important.

One such quilt, whose maker is unknown, has prickly pear cactus, an Indian in leather-fringed leggings and full feathered headdress, and

the logo of the Southern Pacific Railroad embroidered among the more typical birds, butterflies, and fans. Two years, 1875 and 1877, and several sets of initials also appear, as do the words Viva La Independencia and Nogales, A.T. (Arizona Territory).

Another example is an outstanding Crazy quilt reportedly made in Prescott, Arizona. All that is known about the quiltmaker is that she may have been an aunt of Guy Sutherland (manager of the Cotton Land Cattle Company in Mohave County on the Arizona side of the Colorado River). An excellent example of elaborate stitching, it features a fan pattern in each corner; the year 1890 is prominently embroidered in its center. As was the fashion, political ribbons were elements of the ornate blocks. Grover Cleveland is pictured on one, while another promotes the presidential-vice presidential team of Harrison and Morton and is embellished with an eagle and U.S. flag. The maker was evidently fairminded: Cleveland and Harrison were rivals in the 1888 presidential election.

The velvet, satin, and silk patchwork was also embroidered with figures of fish, flowers, a rooster, owl, butterflies, quarter moon, heart, musical notes, anchor, a cross, six-point stars, and a small white house. A wide border embroidered with a variety of vivid chenille flowers ranging from fuchsias to roses, surrounds ornate patchwork.

ABOVE: *Detail of embroidered words "Viva La Independencia," also flowers, umbrella, and initials "F.H.C." with anchor and cross (upside down).*

LEFT: *Crazy quilt, maker unknown, Arizona Territory, c. 1887; pieced, appliquéd and embroidered velvet, silk, and taffeta, 62" x 79."*
Collection of Arizona Historical Society, Southern Arizona Division Museum

OPPOSITE: *Detail of embroidered prickly pear cactus.*

Crazy quilt, made by aunt of Charles Guy Sutherland, Prescott, Arizona, dated 1890; pieced, appliquéd, and embroidered, velvet, satin, and silk, 74" x 80."

Collection of Arizona Historical Society, Southern Arizona Division Museum

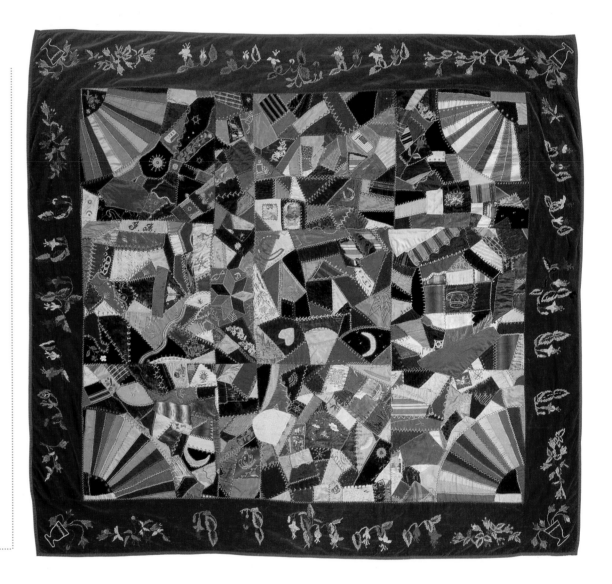

ABOVE: Katherine Daniels Kitt with Papago Indian friends, Papago Reservation, c. 1920.
Courtesy Arizona Historical Society Library

LEFT: Crazy quilt, made by Katherine Daniels Kitt (1876–1945), Tucson, Arizona, 1910; pieced and appliquéd, silk, velvet, and commemorative ribbons, 69" x 83."
Courtesy Mr. and Mrs. Thomas H. Peterson, Jr.

OVERLEAF: Katherine Daniels Kitt painting a desert landscape near Tucson, c. 1900.
Courtesy Arizona Historical Society Library

Although the quiltmaker's identity was not always included, the name or initials of the person a quilt was made to
honor was recorded. A Crazy quilt made in 1910 by Katherine
Daniels Kitt appears to have been made for Katherine's husband, William Roskruge Kitt. The initials W.R.K. are boldly
embroidered in a block on the top row of the quilt, which also
contains numerous ribbons dating from 1901 to 1909, com-
memorating meetings of organizations in Phoenix, Prescott,
and Tucson.

The Kitt family, which had a Tucson dry-goods business
for more than three decades, was active in the commercial
growth of the city, helping to found the Tucson Chamber of
Commerce, Kiwanis, Rotary Club and the Tucson Merchant's
Association. Kitt Peak, west of Tucson, was named by Pima
County surveyor George Roskruge for his sister Philippa

Roskruge Kitt.

Katherine
Daniels, born in 1876
in Chico, California,
studied art in France
and Spain and came
to Tucson in the
1890s to teach art at
the old Safford School. In 1899, she married Will Kitt, son of
William and Philippa. In 1924, she was hired to teach art at the
University of Arizona, where she was instrumental in establishing Art as a department separate from Home Economics.

As an artist, Katherine was fascinated by the Arizona desert
and the Indian people. Over thirty years she came to know the
Papago people well, writing down many of their traditional stories. Her collection of Papago legends, with her illustrations,
was printed in a 1929 book called *Long Ago Told.*

In making her Crazy quilt, Katherine Kitt followed the
honored woman's tradition of doing "fancywork," while
at the same time utilizing her aesthetic training. Quilting fulfilled a desire to make uses of scraps that might otherwise be
thrown away, it made an artistic statement, and was congruent
with the Victorian need to make constructive use of a woman's
"idle" time.

ART AND COMMERCE

In the tradition of using "found" materials, women often incorporated ribbons that were tied around cigars in their fancywork. Tobacco companies were aware of this creative use of
cigar ribbons, and about 1900, two new tobacco advertising
cloths, cigarette silks and cigar flannels, were introduced to

ABOVE: Josephene Elizabeth Maldonado,
Pomona, California, c. 1895.
Courtesy Arizona Historical Society Library

LEFT: Tobacco Flannels quilt made by
Josephene Elizabeth Maldonado Speed
(1876 – 1968), Willcox, Arizona, c. 1915;
machine-pieced and tied cotton tobacco
advertising flannels, 56" x 75."
Collection of Arizona Historical Society, Southern
Arizona Division Museum

help sell tobacco products. (Not coincidentally, this was a time when tobacco companies were actively encouraging women to smoke.)

The silks were usually made of satin, with colorful lithographed designs similar to those women had been using in their Crazy quilts: flags, butterflies, flowers, animals, and birds. Beautiful women and famous people also provided decorative subject matter. Made in series, with a great number of series available, silks featuring flags were most popular. State flags, flags of other nations, and flags with pictures of rulers in the foreground, were highly sought after.

Cigar flannels were produced in fewer series, but like cigarette silks, they most commonly featured flags. There was also an Indian blanket series and an Oriental rug series. While tobacco inserts agree internationally used, these flannel inserts were issued only in the United States.

Collecting complete series of tobacco advertising cloths was a popular hobby, and stitching them into quilts was an effective way to display a collection. Most often, they were simply sewn in rows on a backing fabric.

One Arizona woman who stitched cigar flannels into a quilt was Josephene Speed in Willcox. Josephene Elizabeth Maldonado was born in 1876 in Los Angeles and came to Arizona sometime before 1900, the year she married William Speed, a Texan, in Tucson. The Speeds lived in Willcox, where William was a constable.

In 1906, William, or Billy as he was known, was accepted as an Arizona Ranger. Formed in 1901, the group was modeled after the Texas Rangers. Then thirty-five years old, Billy Speed was the first married man allowed in the company. In 1908, Billy Speed shot and killed Bill Downing, at Downing's business, the Free and Easy Saloon in Willcox. The captain of the Rangers, Harry Wheeler, informed the governor that Downing was "the last of the professional badmen in this section." The Rangers were so effective in curtailing crime that Wheeler soon reported "there has been absolutely no trouble of any kind and I am getting tired of so much goodness as are all the men." The following year, the Rangers were disbanded.

Following Billy's death in 1926, Josephene Speed worked as a hotel clerk in Winkelman, a small mining town along the San Pedro River. The Tobacco Flannel quilt made by Josephine features primarily Indian-motif flannels arranged around a center row of flag flannels that she collected in southern Arizona.

Although tobacco companies stopped including the inserts in 1917, possibly because of the expense, World War I marked the beginning of a quilt revival spurred by patriotism. The U.S.

government encouraged quiltmaking and the slogan, "Make quilts save the blankets for our boys over there," appeared in many magazines and newspapers. Quilt groups made quilts for the Red Cross, and some used their stitchery to raise money for organizations.

SIGNED WITH STITCHES

The use of needlework skills to raise funds for ambitious projects has a long history; women have helped build hospitals, churches, schools, and libraries through such efforts. By recording the signatures of those who donated to a cause, these women also recorded the history of their communities.

The Red Cross quilt made in Phoenix in 1918 is a political and social "time capsule" in fabric of the city and state. It contains the embroidered names of then-Governor George W.P. Hunt, U.S. Senator Mark A. Smith, Secretary of State Sidney P. Osborn, Mayor Peter Corpstein, City Manager V.A. Thompson, and Chief of Police George Brisbois. Banks and numerous other businesses, such as O'Malley Lumber, Barrows Furniture, Crystal Ice & Cold Storage, Sugar Bowl, Switzer Style Shops, and Coca Cola Co. are also memorialized.

Created by the Pythian Sisters (the women's auxiliary of the Knights of Pythias organization), the quilt was made as a

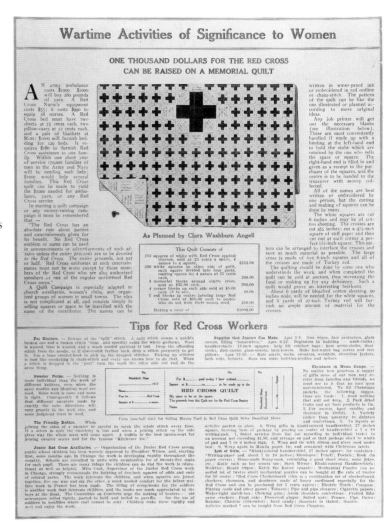

December 1917 issue of The Modern Priscilla *with instructions on how to make a Red Cross fundraising quilt.*

Courtesty Cuesta Benberry

fundraiser for the Red Cross, and exactly duplicates a design presented in the December 1917 issue of *The Modern Priscilla.* The article, titled "Wartime Activities of Significance to Women," pictured and explained a prototype quilt planned by Clara Washburn Angell.

The article suggested that by selling squares or spaces with the name of the contributor embroidered thereon, a total of one thousand dollars could be raised. The spaces throughout the quilt were priced at twenty-five cents; larger, more prominent areas in the center cost from five to twenty-five dollars. The article went on to say that the finished quilt could be auctioned for additional income. It also noted that "such a quilt would make an interesting heirloom."

Eva Cisney, a grand officer in the Purity Temple No.9, is believed to have coordinated the making of the Phoenix Red Cross quilt. Although all signatures are expertly embroidered, apparently by one person, the quilting was done by several hands, perhaps at a quilting bee. It is known that she removed some of the poor quilting and redid some areas that had knots on the back. Eva's husband Claude was presumably the highest bidder on the finished quilt. Their daughters, Grace Cisney Aubineau and Florence Cisney Thompson, donated the quilt to the Arizona Historical Society in the 1970s.

On a smaller, more personal level, many quilts chronicled friendships. The custom of recording names on a "friendship" quilt is an old one. A pattern with a white space in the center where a name could be written was usually chosen. Names were often embroidered and sometimes dates and brief messages were added. Like other quilting activities, the Friendship quilt saw a burst of popularity in the 1930s.

Ethelene Scott Bailey quilted with the Mormon Relief Society in Pomerene. Whenever anyone had a birthday, each woman made a block and embroidered her name on it. The set of blocks was enough for a full quilt and was given to the one celebrating her birthday. Made of pastel scraps, Ethelene's friendship quilt from 1935 preserves memories of friends and the town of Pomerene where she grew up.

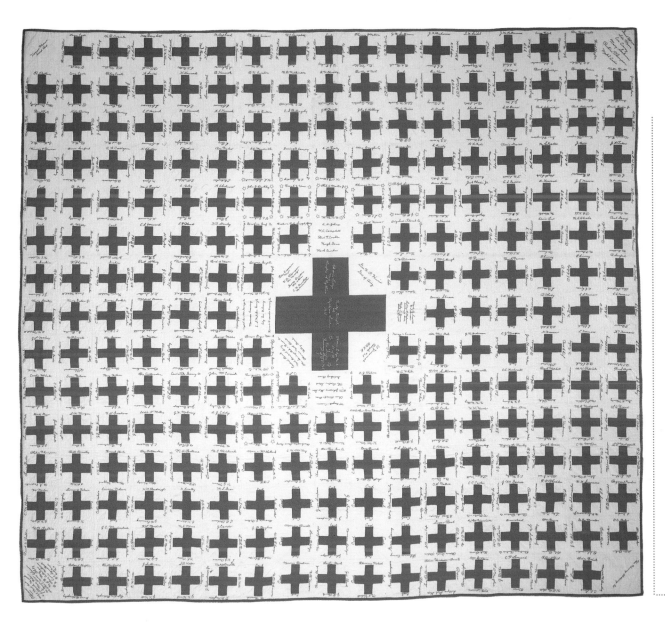

LEFT: Red Cross quilt made by the Pythian Sisters as a fundraiser for the Red Cross during World War I, Phoenix, 1918; machine-pieced and appliquéd cotton, embroidered with signatures, 84" x 95."
Collection of Arizona Historical Society, Central Arizona Division Museum

OPPOSITE: Quilting Bee in Pomerene, Arizona, c. 1940.
Courtesy Ethelene Scott Bailey

ABOVE: *Ethelene Scott (1912–),*
Tempe, Arizona, 1931.
Courtesy Ethelene Scott Bailey

RIGHT: *Friendship Album quilt made by*
friends of Ethelene Scott Bailey, Mormon
Relief Society, Pomerene, Arizona, 1935;
pieced cotton with embroidered signatures
and dates, 70" x 82."
Courtesy Ethelene Scott Bailey

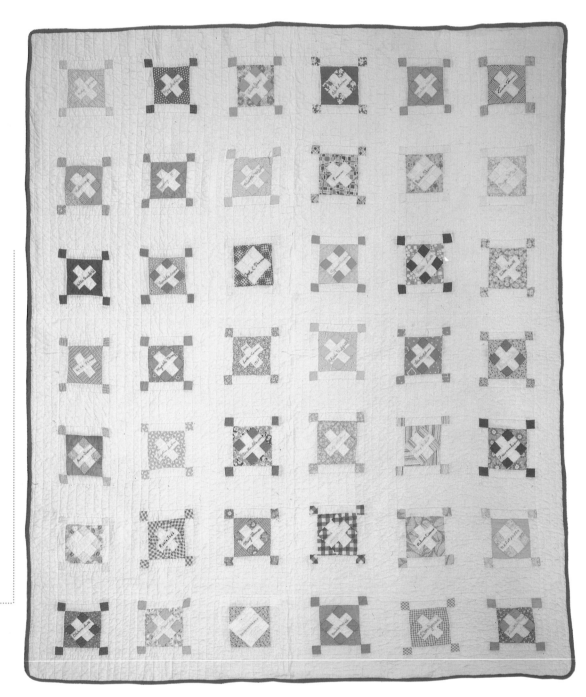

ABOVE: Pincushion made from a slice of yucca stalk, McNeal, Arizona, c. 1930.
Courtesy Dorothea Littleton

LEFT: Friendship Album quilt made by Frontier Homemakers group, McNeal, Arizona, 1939; appliquéd cotton feed sacks, 64" x 77."
Courtesy Dorothea Littleton

Located just north of Benson in southern Arizona, the town of Pomerene was founded in 1912 by Mormon families abandoning homes and farms in Mexico as they fled from Pancho Villa and his troops during the Mexican Revolution. Ethelene was born that same year in the town of Douglas, to parents who were among the missionaries leaving Mexico and crossing the border into Arizona. Ethelene remembers quilting as part of her daily life as a girl. "I don't know how old I was when I started quilting, but my mother always had a quilt hanging in the ceiling." With twelve children, the family used a lot of quilts. "Some of her quilts were tied, but most of them were quilted because they lasted longer quilted."

Church women made up the most common quilting groups, but sometimes membership was more diverse. One unusual group counted several men among its members. The Frontier Homemakers consisted of men and women from neighboring ranches near McNeal in southeastern Arizona who met regularly. Whoever had a quilt top ready would place it in the frames before the others arrived; stopping only for the noon meal, which was potluck, the group would usually have the top "quilted out" by afternoon.

When Dorothea Littleton became engaged to her husband Leroy in 1939, the group made a Friendship Album quilt for the couple. The blocks, of colorful flour and feed sacks, feature signatures from Dorothea's teacher and the mayor of Bisbee, as well as those of family and friends.

FAMILY TRADITIONS

In some families, not only quilts but the tradition of quiltmaking has been passed down for generations. Laura Saline in Taylor, Arizona, treasures her family's four-generation quilting tradition. Laura learned to piece when she made some small, four-patch blocks when she was just six. This was the beginning of a lifetime of making quilts, carrying on the family tradition of fine needlework.

This tradition began with Dianna Greer Camp, born in Tennessee in 1806. One of her favorite quilt designs was Democratic Victory (also known as Whigs Defeat) popular in the middle of the nineteenth century. After she and her husband, William Washington Camp, a minister, converted to the Mormon faith they moved to Nauvoo, Illinois, where the church was at that time headquartered.

When persecution of the Mormons prompted the migration to Utah, the Camp family also traveled West, arriving in the Salt Lake Valley in 1850. Their fifteenth child, Margaret Henrietta Camp, was born as they left Nauvoo in 1848. An early infection

*ABOVE: Margaret Henrietta Camp Baird
with her daughter, Laura, and grandchildren on her front porch, Snowflake,
Arizona, c 1910.*
Courtesy Laura H. Saline

*LEFT: Democratic Victory/Whig's Defeat
quilt made by Margaret Henrietta Camp
Baird (1848–1941), Concho, Arizona,
between 1890 and 1910; pieced and
appliquéd cotton, 69" x 82."*
Courtesy Laura H. Saline

crippled Margaret but, because of her handicap, she was given an excellent education, receiving her schooling in the Lion House alongside the children of President Brigham Young.

Margaret married Thomas Burgess Brantley, a Confederate Army veteran, in 1866; when he died from an old war wound within two years, Margaret was left with an infant son. She later married Richard Alexander Baird, a young widower introduced to her by Brigham Young, and they became the parents of seven children—the youngest born three weeks after Richard's death in 1882.

A widow with eight children, Margaret made preparations to join her sister, Ellen Camp Greer, in Concho, Arizona. Her oldest son, Tom Brantley, drove one of the wagons on the trip, crossing the Little Colorado at Lee's Ferry. Arriving in Concho, Margaret found that her sister was also a widow. The two women lived together for a time and supported their families by making and selling butter and repairing clothes for the "great strings of cowboys" in the area. After moving to St. Johns four years later, Margaret taught music lessons, using the piano she brought with her on the long trip from Utah. When a wrist injury prevented her from playing the piano, she turned to quiltmaking.

Margaret was an excellent seamstress and enjoyed doing "fancy hand work." She made several quilts in the Democratic Victory design, copying one of her mother's favorite patterns. She also made more than one Star design. Margaret's daughter, Laura Gertrude Baird, was just two years old when the family came to Arizona Territory in 1882. After an early marriage ended in divorce, Laura and her three children moved to Snowflake, where she attended Snowflake Stake Academy. There she met Alma Hunt, whose offer of marriage she refused, saying she "would rather be an old man's sweetheart than a young man's slave." She later graduated from Northern Arizona Normal School, receiving her teaching certificate. Laura taught the primary grades and was known as an innovative and gifted instructor.

Laura's romance with Alma Hunt was rekindled when she returned a lost saddle blanket to him; by this time, he was a recent widower with six children. He married Laura in 1919, and their daughter—also named Laura—was born the following year. Through the years, they opened their home to forty foster children.

To support his family, Alma worked part-time as a freighter, driving a wagon and team between Fort Apache and Holbrook, Arizona. About 1920, Laura's aunt Ellen gave him a colorful scrap quilt to keep him warm on these long trips. A

Lone Star quilt made by Margaret Henrietta
Camp Baird (1848–1941), Snowflake,
Arizona, c. 1930; pieced cotton, 63" x 77."
Courtesy Laura H. Saline

variation of the traditional Bethlehem Star pattern, the quilt was called a Freighter Quilt by the family.

In addition to making intricate pieced quilts, the women of the Camp-Baird-Hunt-Saline family enjoyed displaying their delicate quilting in whole-cloth quilts. Laura Hunt made a blue satin quilt with pink satin backing for a birthday gift. The quilt, featuring elaborate quilting in a design hand-drawn on the quilt by a friend in Taylor, won a first place ribbon at the local county fair in 1940. Laura also made a similar whole-cloth quilt she called the Sweetheart Quilt because she made so many as wedding gifts.

Making baby quilts was also a family tradition. In 1942, Laura Hunt's daughter, Laura Hunt Saline, made a beautifully quilted, pale blue whole-cloth quilt, edged with blue lace crocheted by her mother for the birth of her first child.

The family raised sheep and used their wool for most of their quilt batts until the mid-thirties. They sheared the sheep, washed and carded the wool. Laura Saline remembers the adults gathering around the fireplace to card wool for batting. The children helped by removing debris from the wool; Laura recalls that if the children were especially good, they were rewarded by being allowed to walk barefoot on the batts on the floor. They sometimes purchased cotton batts, but these were used sparingly because of the cost.

In some instances, the tradition of family needlework was not passed from mother to daughter but from mother-in-law to daughter-in-law. Such appears to be the case with Bessie McKinney Rhodes and Mary Freeman Rhodes.

Bessie Pearl McKinney was only ten years old when her mother's illness resulted in the family's leaving Texas and moving to Arizona in 1893. Making the journey in a covered wagon, the family settled in the fertile San Pedro Valley. Within a few years of her mother's death, Bessie married and became the mother of three sons. Divorce later ended the marriage. In 1910, she met and married John Tewksbury Rhodes, only son of John Tewskbury, who was killed in the infamous feud between the Graham and Tewksbury families that became known as the Pleasant Valley War.

John's mother Mary Ann Tewksbury was pregnant with her second child when her husband John was shot and killed near their home on Cherry Creek. She witnessed the murder from inside the cabin, but attempts by Mary Ann to retrieve the bodies of John and his friend were met with gunfire. According to reports, each night she crept out and covered the bodies with quilts weighted down with rocks to protect them from half-wild hogs, which foraged along Cherry Creek.

*Bethlehem Star Variation quilt made by
Ellen Camp Greer (1837–1929), Concho,
Arizona, c. 1920; pieced cotton, 72" x 78."*

Courtesy Laura H. Saline

Whole Cloth quilt made by Laura Baird
Hunt (1880–1985), Taylor, Arizona,
1939; rayon satin whole cloth, 80" x 96."
Courtesy Laura H. Saline

Whole Cloth Baby Quilt made by Laura Hunt Saline (1920–), Pima, Arizona, 1942; rayon whole cloth with hand crocheted lace edge, 41" x 52."

Courtesy Laura H. Saline

After eleven days, authorities finally arrived to restore peace and bury the bodies. Less than a month later, Mary Ann gave birth to a son and named him John. She later married John Rhodes, another participant in the feud, and her son John Tewksbury added Rhodes to his own name.

John and Bessie Rhodes homesteaded in the Galiuro Mountains, near Mammoth, Arizona, and became the parents of two sons. The ranch was isolated, with no electricity. Because there was less to do in the winter, this time was used to make quilts. When her younger son Thomas married in 1935, Bessie pieced a Double T quilt as a gift for him and his bride Mary Freeman. The "T" most likely was for Thomas but it could also stand for Tewksbury. The quilt makes a strong graphic impression, with the blue Double T blocks set on point, and solid pink sashing between the blocks creating a "streak of lightning" effect.

Bessie later divorced John, but continued to run the ranch by herself. She is remembered as a strong-willed woman, one who kept a "tidy house" with quilts on all the beds. Bessie Rhodes and her daughter-in-law Mary Freeman Rhodes may have quilted together at the ranch. In addition to their quilting, Bessie and Mary Rhodes shared a number of similarities: both were from pioneer families, both were independent women, and both were divorced twice.

Mary Freeman met Bessie and Tom Rhodes as a child, after the Freeman family arrived in Arizona in 1915 to claim the last homestead in Pima County. Like many ranch families, they lived in Tucson during the school year, and the Freeman and Rhodes children attended school together.

In 1935, when Mary Freeman married Tom Rhodes, they received the Double T quilt made by Bessie Rhodes. The young couple made their home with Tom's parents, and perhaps this is when Mary learned to quilt. She loved needlework of all kinds and made a Garden Bouquet appliqué quilt in the 1930s. The flowers and blue birds came from newpaper patterns. Published in the "Nancy Page Quilt Club" syndicated column, the pattern included a series of twenty different flowers. Mary also made an appliqué alphabet quilt for her first child.

ABOVE: Rhodes family (right to left: John, Johnny, Bessie, Tom) at the Grand Canyon, c. 1925.
Courtesy John & Theresa Rhodes

LEFT: Double "T" quilt made by Bessie Pearl McKinney Rhodes (1878–1966), Sombero Butte, Arizona, 1935; pieced cotton and lightweight wool chambray, 59" x 78."
Courtesy John and Theresa Rhodes

OPPOSITE: Garden Bouquet quilt (detail) made by Mary Josephine Freeman Rhodes (1917–1987), Sombrero Butte, Arizona, c. 1935; pieced cotton, 70" x 85."
Courtesy John and Theresa Rhodes

In some cases, the completion of a single quilt took so much time that it became a family tradition. Such is the case with a red, white, and blue Feathered Star quilt now owned by Cherrel Weech of Safford. Her great-grandmother, Nancy Oliver, pieced red-and-white Feathered Star blocks in 1903 in Eden, Arizona, when her daughter, Rilla Ann Oliver Curtis, was expecting her first child. She gave the blocks to her daughter, but the quilt was never completed. Rilla Ann, in turn, gave the blocks

to her daughter, Laura Curtis Batty, born in 1904. Laura, Nancy's granddaughter, finally stitched the blocks together and quilted the Feathered Star quilt in 1938.

Nancy Francis Lovern Oliver was born in 1839 in Illinois, and Nancy crossed the plains with the Mormon migration to the Salt Lake Valley. She married William Temple Oliver in Utah in 1856; as a young family, the Olivers pioneered various settlements in Utah and Arizona. Their thirteenth child was born after arriving in the settlement of Show Low, Arizona. In 1888, the Olivers settled in the Gila Valley. There William became the first postmaster of the town and gave it the name Eden.

TO WARM A CHILD

Family event quilts were tangible mileposts in life for individuals as well as for generations. Of these, quilts made to celebrate the arrival of a baby were the most common. While some were used and "loved to death," others become cherished heirlooms; both are important.

During the nineteenth century, quilts made for babies and children were scaled-down versions of their larger counterparts. Later, special patterns were promoted for children's quilts, and twentieth-century women began the practice of using pastel colors for baby quilts.

Baby quilts were sometimes made by the new mother, but often these small, sweet coverings were stitched as an expression of love and concern by a grandmother. One

ABOVE: *Laura Curtis Batty, Eden, Arizona, c. 1925.*
Courtesy Cherrel Batty Weech

LEFT: *Feathered Star quilt made over 30 years by three generations, Nancy Frances Oliver (1839–1925), Rilla Ann Oliver Curtis (1876–1947), Laura Curtis Batty (1904–1958), Eden/Pima, Arizona, 1903–1938; pieced cotton, 68" x 84."*
Courtesy Cherrel Batty Weech

OPPOSITE: *Nancy Frances Oliver (center), Eden, Arizona, c. 1910.*
Courtesy Cherrel Batty Weech

such grandmother sent a note with the quilt she made for her daughter's son Dell in 1903:

This quilt is for Dell. If his life is as tuff as the living god pitty him. I like to a never got it quilted it was just tuff job but maybe it will help to turn the cold wind. Think over me when you see it.

A lonely mother

Sarah Jane Whitmer created a Sunbonnet Sue and Overall Sam baby quilt in 1940 for her unborn granddaughter Jennie. She made it special by adding appliqué flowers to Sue's hat; two of the Sue figures carry umbrellas, while two of the Sam figures have balloons. Details were added to the figures with embroidery.

Born in the Mormon community of Pima in 1884, Sarah Jane Judd was the first child of pioneers who had come from Utah to settle in Arizona. Her father called her Jennie and, at an early age, she learned to cook, sew, and help her mother. Quilting was part of their daily life. Sarah married Angus Van Meter Whitmer in 1901, and they settled in the White Mountain community of Alpine. Sarah had thirteen children; during the long snowy winters, she and her daughters kept busy making quilts to provide warm bedding for the large family.

Sarah sewed most of the family's clothes and ordered material through Sears catalog or purchased it at Becker's Mercantile Store in Springerville. She saved her scraps in a large box, and two sisters, living nearby in New Mexico, sent her all theirs as well. It was from this box of scraps that Sarah stitched Sunbonnet Sue and Overall Sam on the baby quilt.

In addition to the many practical quilts Sarah made for her family, she also quilted with a church group called the Aunt Dianas. They made quilts for church benefits and family gifts. Sarah's granddaughter Jennie remembers that as a child, she often went with her mother and grandmother to the weekly meetings of the Aunt Dianas in one of the member's homes. While the women quilted, Jennie helped by threading needles and picking up scraps from the floor.

Baby quilts, frequently made while a mother-to-be was waiting for the birth of a child or shortly after a baby was born, were sometimes also included in a young girl's hope chest. When her daughter Alice became engaged in 1937, Frances Fairbanks of Phoenix made a Four-Pointed Star, or Periwinkle baby quilt, for her future grandchildren, using a wide assortment of scraps to create a colorful field of twinkling stars.

John and Frances Johnson Fairbanks came to Phoenix in 1913 when there were vast desert areas between towns in the

ABOVE: Sarah Jane Whitmer and husband, Angus, with granddaughter, Jennie, c. 1940.
Courtesy Jennie Campbell

LEFT: Sunbonnet Sue & Overall Sam quilt made by Sarah Jane Judd Whitmer (1884–1967), Alpine, Arizona, 1940; appliquéd cotton, 25" x 37."
Courtesy Jennie Campbell

Salt River Valley. The Fairbanks and their three-year-old daughter Alice Jean came to Arizona from Washington state to be near Frances' family. Frances Johnson had graduated from the University of Washington in 1902 as a registered nurse, but in Phoenix she was a homemaker. John Fairbanks, a survivor of the great San Francisco earthquake, worked after the quake restringing telephone lines in San Francisco. In Phoenix, he got a job with Mountain Bell, where he worked for forty-five years. Frances did not have a sewing machine until the 1940s, and so did all of her sewing by hand; the Periwinkle baby quilt was presumably pieced this way.

The chronicles in cloth cherished by generations tell us more than just the facts they record. We can touch the scraps of fabric—coarse feed sacks or elegant velvets—and feel a connection to our ancestors. We can see the stitches they made—tiny and delicate or large and strong—and know a bit more about the women who came before and the events of their daily lives.

However, there have always been a few quilts that are set apart from daily life. Their makers took traditional patterns beyond the ordinary and stitched creations of their own imagination. Such quilts entered the realm of art.

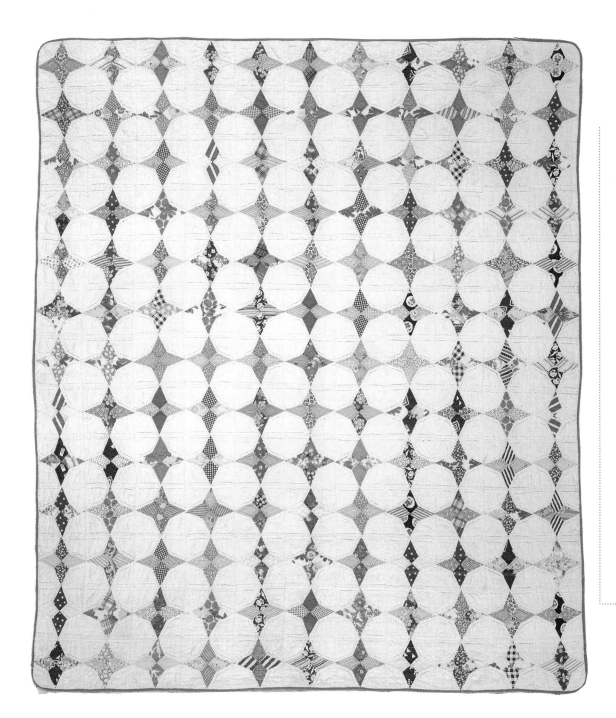

*Periwinkle quilt made by Frances Johnson
Fairbanks (1880–1965), Phoenix, 1937;
pieced cotton, 43" x 51."*
Courtesy Mrs. Barbara Resides

Detail of Desert Appliqué block shows delicately embroidered flowers on cactus and embroidery snake.

Also shows swastika design quilted in borders.

BEYOND THE ORDINARY

Quilts as Art

Emma's scrapbook where she kept detailed records of each quilt she made, including information about the source of her designs, swatches of fabric, correspondence regarding her quilts, photographs, and records of any awards she won.

Courtesy Mark & Jill Tetreau

S ome quilts were intended to be works of art rather than ordinary bedcovers. And some quiltmakers were more truly artists than ordinary seamstresses. The artistic talents of a number of Arizona quilters are reflected in their handstitched masterpieces—quilts that are beyond the ordinary. Arizona quilt artisans such as Rose Livingston, Nellie Smith, and Emma Andres used their eye for beauty and design, along with their needlework skills, to take quiltmaking beyond the ordinary into the realm of art.

ARTISTS WITH A NEEDLE

Nellie von Gerichten Smith was said to be the first woman to play violin with the San Francisco Philharmonic Orchestra. As the wife of Barney Smith she came to Prescott, Arizona, at the turn of the century. Inspired by her adopted home, Nellie wrote and published musical scores with titles such as "A Storm in the Grand Canyon" and "Song of the Pines." She also gave music lessons to the children of Prescott and wrote children's books and poems.

Chaperoned by her mother, Nellie sometimes entertained at her husband's business, the Palace Bar on the main street of Prescott. The infamous Palace Bar was destroyed by fire in July of 1900. (It was rebuilt the next year of brick and stone and remains a landmark in downtown Prescott today.) From the Palace, Nellie Smith collected hundreds of tiny blue silk ribbons that came tied around the necks of Pabst Blue Ribbon beer bottles between 1895 and 1914 . She stitched the ribbons together in a Tumbling Block pattern, displaying her artistic flair and needlework skill by embroidering over the seams with red-and-white feather stitches, which created an overall pattern of white stars separated by red hexagons (the words "Pabst Blue Ribbon" and "Guaranteed Perfect" are still faintly visible on the blue ribbons). This unique work of art is the only "quilt" that Nellie is known to have made.

While Nellie was meticulously stitching tiny blue ribbons in Prescott, Rose Livingston was working as a dressmaker and hatmaker in Yuma, honing the skills that later in her life would blossom into a profusion of color in a series of floral quilts.

In 1880, at age fifteen, Rose Graham came by train from Indiana to Yuma, Arizona, to marry Charles Alderson, a commercial painter she had known in Indiana. When she arrived in Yuma, Rose was one of only a handful of white women in the community. She and Charles had three children when he was killed in a train accident. Rose supported her young family with her skills as a dressmaker and milliner.

Although she married Gus Livingston, sheriff of Territorial Yuma, in 1901, she continued to stitch every day to help support her family, which grew to include one more son. Rose didn't begin to quilt until the 1920s, when she was in her fifties; the national flurry of quiltmaking in the twenties and thirties may have inspired her to use her needlework skills to create her bold, blooming quilts for her grandchildren. All of her quilts are floral appliqué designs that may have been based on the many appliqué designs popularized in newspapers and magazines of the period. Her love of color and refined needlework skills allowed her to adapt these patterns in most extraordinary ways.

ABOVE: Nellie von Gerichten Smith, c. 1890.
Courtesy Sharlot Hall Museum, Prescott

LEFT: Pabst Blue Ribbon quilt made by Nellie von Gerichten Smith (1870–1952), Prescott, Arizona, c. 1910; silk ribbons from Pabst Blue Ribbon beer bottles connected with feather stitch, 77" x 76."
Courtesy Mrs. Carl Jones

ABOVE: Detail of original appliqué flowers shows extraordinary variety of colors and gradual shading gradations within each flower. Also shows delicately embroidered butterflies.

RIGHT: Black Floral quilt made by Rose Graham Livingston (1865–1955), Yuma, Arizona, c. 1930; original design appliquéd cotton and silk with black quilting thread, 86" x 94."

Courtesy Jean Frith

ABOVE: Rose Livingston with youngest son, Yuma, Arizona, c. 1902.
Courtesy Jean Frith

LEFT: Flowering Vine quilt made by Rose Graham Livingston (1865–1955), Yuma, Arizona, c. 1930; appliquéd cotton with embroidery, 94" x 95."
Courtesy Betsy Gottsponer

EVERLASTING BLOOMS

The Flowering Vine quilt contains five vertical vines punctuated with a wide array of flowers, ranging from purple pansies with delicately embroidered centers to stylized zinnias with a dozen shades in the petals of each flower. The quilt's white background enhances the vivid colors of the flowers.

Rose's black floral quilt also features vivid, shaded flowers and embroidered butterflies; it may have been inspired by a design called Roosevelt Rose by Ruth Finley, which appeared in the January 1934 issue of *Good Housekeeping*. That pattern called for a background of black sateen with appliquéd flowers created from tiny yo-yos, or puffs. For her quilt, Rose used her own much more delicate and complex original flowers arranged in an oval on a dramatic black silk background. The quilt has an unusual red cotton backing and was quilted with black thread.

A unique Miniature Dahlia quilt was made while Rose was recovering from a fall that broke both her legs. Using the appliqué skills she had perfected in making the large floral quilts, she stitched miniature dahlias in thirty-nine, four-and-one-half-inch blocks that she made on her lap. She then set the dahlia blocks on point alternately with solid peach fabric.

Rose took great pride and pleasure in doing all of the fine appliqué work on the colorful quilt tops, but was not interested in doing the actual quilting, and so they were quilted by a Yuma Mormon Relief Society.

AN ARIZONA ORIGINAL

At least one quilt artisan, Anna Walahart Andres, passed on not only quilts but also her needlework talent and eye for design to her daughter, Emma Andres. A Crazy quilt, with delicate embroidery on velvet and silk, is just one example of Anna Walahart Andres's exceptional needlework skills. She began the quilt in 1895, when she was sixteen, collecting silk and taffeta pieces from various sources, including young men whom she convinced to give her their ties. Embroidery thread was an expensive component; she used "over $15 worth of silk thread ...bought on small spools with Mama's spending money." The quilt contains a wide assortment of embroidered designs, figures, and flowers. In addition, it preserves numerous printed ribbons, one of which reads "Central City, Colorado, July 4, 1895."

Anna was born in Switzerland in 1879 and came to the United States as a small child. Her family settled in Colorado, where her father owned a saloon. Anna wanted to become a teacher, but instead had to leave school early and do domestic work for other families. Her quilt, with the embroidered initials

Miniature Dahlia quilt made by Rose Graham Livingston (1865–1955), Yuma, Arizona, c. 1930; appliquéd cotton, 85" x 87."

Courtesy Marjorie Ewing

A.W. and M.A., was finished just before her marriage, in 1898, to Matthew Andres. Shortly thereafter, they travelled to Arizona and established a cigar factory in the capital city of Prescott. Anna sewed for all of her five children, instilling in them a love of beauty and appreciation of good workmanship.

These qualities were especially adopted by her daughter, Emma. Born in 1902, Emma spent after-school hours helping in her father's store. Following high school graduation, she worked at the cigar store full-time, where she spent quiet time reading the magazines and newspapers the store stocked. Quilt patterns and articles were printed regularly at the time, and Emma read all of them.

A scrapbook enthusiast, Emma kept detailed records of each quilt she made, including information about the source of her designs, any awards they won, swatches of fabric, and photographs of the finished quilts. She also collected articles on quilting and handwork and maintained extensive correspondence with many other quiltmakers of that time. After the publication of quilting books by Carrie Hall and Florence Peto in the 1930s, Emma began a correspondence with both women that lasted throughout their lives. The letters exchanged were full of quilting news, and sometimes included photos or samples of works in progress and gifts of fabric.

Intrigued with an ad in a women's magazine in 1931, Emma made an appliqué quilt from a mail-order kit, pieced a second quilt, and began a third of her own design. That quilt, which had tiny red and white squares that formed a silhouette of a woman spinning, won a merit award in the 1933 Sears, Roebuck, & Company "Century of Progress" quilt contest.

Emma spent over a year designing and making her next original quilt, "Out Where the West Begins." She embroidered a verse from a poem by Arthur Chapman and surrounded it with blocks of appliquéd desert mountains and cactus. Each block also includes a tiny embroidered snake. Emma used a swastika motif for the border quilting because this shape was frequently woven into Navajo blankets and baskets. An ancient symbol with multiple meanings, the swastika represents the four directions of the universe and denotes a progression of travel from ignorance to wisdom some believe. Southwestern Indian tribes revere it as a symbol of the Great Spirit and use it to signify good luck and friendship. When the quilt was displayed at a state fair during the war years, Emma wrote in her scrapbook that she was "under suspicion at Fair" because of this design. She was very indignant that her patriotism would be questioned and collected articles in her scrapbook showing that the swastika was in fact an ancient Indian symbol.

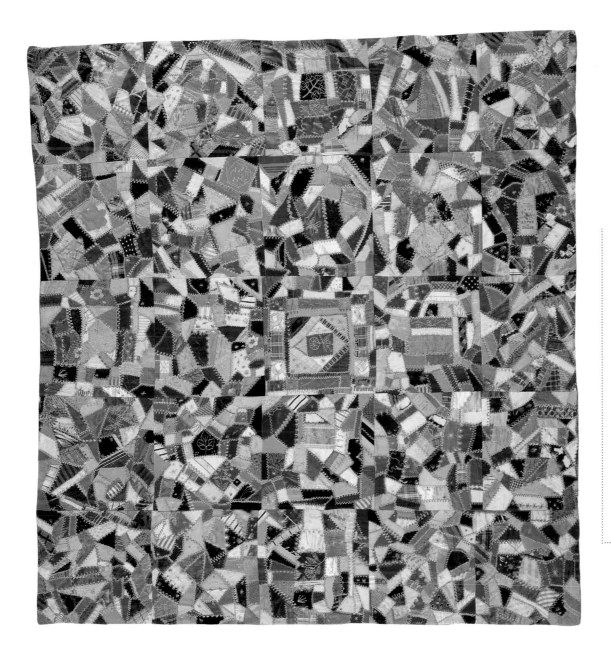

ABOVE: Anna Walahart Andres with daughter, Alice, Prescott, c. 1900.
Courtesy Sister Anna Marcella

LEFT: Crazy quilt made by Anna Walahart Andres (1879–1963), Colorado, 1895; pieced and appliquéd velvet, silk, and various dated ribbon; embroidery of various figures, includes initials "A.W." and "M.A." with date 1895.
Courtesy Mark & Jill Tetreau

Inspired by a quilt in a 1934 issue of *The Home Art Needlework* magazine, Emma used stamped blocks to create her redwork State Flowers quilt. She embroidered the flower and the name of each of the forty-eight states in red on a white background and set the blocks with sashing. A secondary design was formed by adding triangles to the corners of the blocks. Typical of Emma's attention to detail, she dyed her own red fabric so it would exactly match the red embroidery thread. She wrote in her scrapbook that this quilt was "started in 1935 and finished binding March 12, 1938. Finished last block of quilting March 9 at 5:08. Oh! Boy." Encouraged by Peto, Emma

collected ideas, drawings, and research for an Arizona Commemorative quilt. After exchanging several letters with the secretary of state, she obtained a copy of the Great Seal of Arizona. The quilt features an embroidered reproduction of the state seal with the year of statehood, 1912. In a circle at the top of the quilt she embroidered the state bird, a cactus wren, perched near the state flower, a saguaro cactus blossom. Embroidered in a circle at the bottom is the log cabin in Prescott that served as the territory's first capitol.

Emma used a design of Arizona flags to create a dramatic and effective border. The Arizona Commemorative quilt, finished in 1938, garnered the blue ribbon and accompanying cash prize of one dollar and fifty cents at the 1940 Arizona State Fair. She was especially pleased because the quilt, along with "Out Where the West Begins" (which also won a blue ribbon that year), were "the only quilts exhibited that they spread out and pinned up on the wall so the people can see all of each quilt".

Emma also collected some fascinating quilts. In 1942, she purchased a President's Wreath quilt with a mysterious history through Florence Peto. The quilt was one of two made before she was twenty-one by Louisa Kline, a hard-working German farm girl born in Pennsylvania in 1824.

ABOVE: Postcard captioned "Navajos Renounce Their Swastika Design After U.S. Declares War", c. 1940. According to the note on the back of the postcard, the Navajo declaration read:

"Because the above ornament which has been a symbol of friendship among our forefathers for many centuries has been desecrated recently by another nation of people. Therefore it is resolved that henceforth from this date on and forever more our tribes renounce the use of the emblem commonly known today as the swastika or flyfoot on our bankets, baskets, art objects, sandpaintings and clothing."

LEFT: Miniature Grandmother's Flower Garden quilt made by Emma Andres (1902–1987), Prescott, Arizona, 1932; pieced cotton, 31" x 42." This baby quilt contains over 1500 pieces; each measures less than an inch.
Courtesy Mark & Jill Tetreau

OPPOSITE: Emma Andres in her "Happiness Museum," her father's old cigar store on Gurley Street in downtown Prescott, c. 1980.
Courtesy Mark & Jill Tetreau

RIGHT: Desert Appliqué quilt made by Emma Andres (1902–1987), Prescott, Arizona, 1934; original design appliquéd cotton, 69" x 75" Embroidered poem "Out Where The West Begins" by Arthur Chapman reads:

"Out where the handclasp's a little stronger,
Out where the smile dwells a little longer,
That's where the West begins,
Out where the sun is a little brighter,
Where the snows that fall are a trifle whiter,
Where the bonds of home are a wee bit tighter,
That's where the West begins."

Courtey Mark & Jill Tetreau

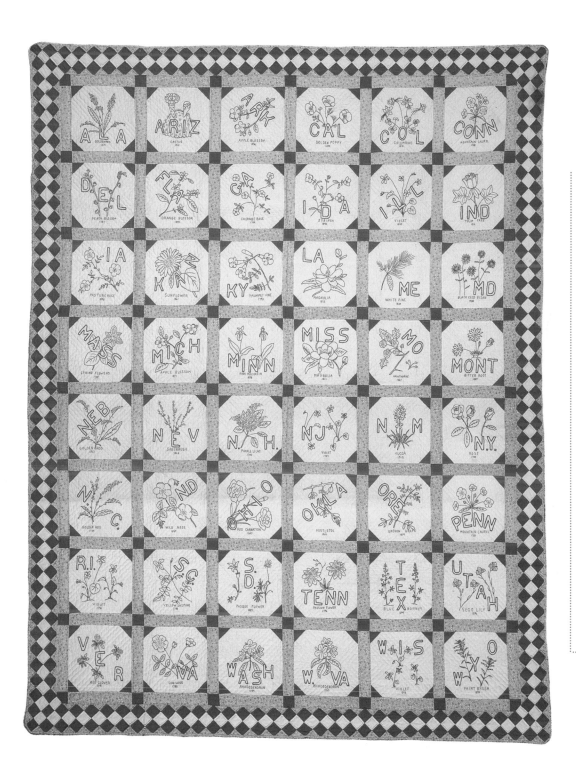

Redwork State Flowers quilt made by
Emma Andres (1902–1987), Prescott,
Arizona, 1938; pieced and embroidered
cotton, 62" x 80."
Courtesy Mark & Jill Tetreau

According to Florence Peto, in her 1939 book *Historic Quilts*, "All the work on the quilts was done by candlelight during long winter evenings and on Saturday afternoons, her one recreation period, at which time Louisa was excused from helping with farm duties."

The President's Wreath pattern, one of many variations on a Wreath-of-Roses theme, was popular as a bridal quilt. Not heeding the superstitious belief that using hearts on a quilt before one was actually engaged was bad luck, Louisa quilted

four hearts in each red calico rose. At twenty-one, Louisa became engaged and announced her wedding date to her friends. On the day of the wedding, friends and family arrived at the Kline farm, but the groom did not. After several hours a search was begun, but the disappearance of the young groom on his wedding day remained an unsolved mystery. Louisa never married, and the quilt was never used. In the center wreath of the quilt there is a carefully concealed patch, and it was speculated that Louisa may have removed names and dates that were stitched into the quilt.

After her death at age eighty-three, Louisa Kline's quilt was passed on to a niece. Florence Peto included the quilt and its poignant story in her book and, through her, Emma purchased the President's Wreath.

Another quilt Emma purchased through Florence Peto was her Lemon Star quilt. Emma's name for the quilt came from her pronunciation of the pattern known as LeMoyne Star, an early pattern named for Jean Baptiste and Pierre LeMoyne, who founded New Orleans in 1718. Emma's Lemon Star is a delightful variation on that pattern: eight diamonds that form a star.

Although the maker of the quilt is unknown, strong pinks and greens are typical of quilts made by people of German descent known as Pennsylvania Dutch. The quilt was hand-pieced, with small pink diamonds appliquéd on the blocks. The diagonal setting creates a sophisticated effect. It was then hand-quilted with small, precise stitches around each shape and in a diamond grid on the sashing pieces.

The quiltmaker who originally inspired Emma to make her Silhouette quilt was Charles Pratt. In 1932, she read a newspaper story that included pictures of some of his quilts and explained how he pieced picture quilts from tiny silk squares.

ABOVE: Emma Andres with two of her quilts at exhibit in Prescott, Arizona, c. 1940, (right: Arizona Commemorative, left: Tillman Bouquet).
Courtesy Mark & Jill Tetreau

LEFT: Arizona Commemorative quilt made by Emma Andres (1902–1987), Prescott, Arizona, 1938; original design pieced, appliquéd, and embroidered, 57" x 71."
Courtesy Mark & Jill Tetreau

OPPOSITE: Detail of embroidered Great Seal of the State of Arizona.

President's Wreath quilt, a Rose Wreath Variation, made by Louisa Kline (1824–1907), Harrisburg, Pennsylvania, c. 1845; pieced cottons, 86" x 88." Quilt historian, Florence Peto, described Louisa's quilt as a "miracle of fine quilting. Indeed, this writer has never seen such machine-like precision surpassed on any other quilt; photographs do not do justice to the texture which results from such stitchery."

Courtesy Mark & Jill Tetreau

Eight-Pointed Star quilt, quiltmaker
unknown, called Lemon Star by Emma
Andres c. 1860; pieced cottons, 83" x 103."
Courtesy Mark & Jill Tetreau

Fascinated by his designs, Emma dreamed of getting to know him. When she read another story about him in 1940, in the *Philadelphia Inquirer,* she made an effort to obtain his address. She wrote to him, he answered, and they began a by-mail friendship. As Emma later wrote, "We surely got to be good pals." Florence Peto was also intrigued when she read about Charles Pratt and was able to contact him through Emma. Pratt was thrilled when Peto displayed his quilts at her lectures.

Charles Pratt was born in Manchester, England, in 1851 and, in 1886, immigrated to the United States, where he settled in Philadelphia, worked as a carpetmaker, and began to design and piece quilts. The patterns he created were made up of thousands of small squares, sometimes less than a half-inch in size, which he arranged into unique pictorials or unusual mosaic designs. He usually used silk fabrics and always pieced by hand. Pratt sewed a backing to the top, envelope-style, but his quilts had no batting and no quilting as they were meant for display rather than for practical use.

Pratt took great pride in his quilts and entered them in competitions. In 1910, he set a goal of winning a blue ribbon from competitions in each of the forty-eight states, a goal he achieved twenty years later. In a fifty-year period, his quilts won more than four hundred ribbons.

Charles Pratt died in 1941 at the age of eighty-nine. Because Emma had had an intense friendship with Pratt, his daughter gave Emma nine of his quilts, including the Oriental Mosaic. Bold in color, design, and effect, the quilt contains twenty thousand, three-eighths-inch squares, given sharp definition by the solid color cotton fabrics.

Always happy to share her love of quilts with others, Emma initiated annual quilt exhibits in the 1940s. Each exhibit had a theme and displayed her quilts, quilts others made and purchased by her, and quilts submitted by invitation from her quilting friends nationwide. Hours were established for viewing, and Emma lectured; all proceeds were donated to a worthy organization. These exhibitions became major cultural events in Prescott.

The forties brought Emma national recognition as well. Not only were her quilts shown on the East Coast and used by Florence Peto in some of her lectures, the November 22, 1942, issue of *Every Week* magazine, a national Sunday newspaper

LEFT: Oriental Mosaic quilt (spelled "Orientel" on the quilt) made by Charles Pratt (1851–1941), Philadelphia, Pennsylvannia, c. 1920; pieced cottons; more than 20,000 3/8-inch squares, 58" x 62."
Courtesy Mark & Jill Tetreau

OPPOSITE: Charles Pratt working on one of his quilts, Philadelphia, 1940. He took pride in the thousands of tiny squares in his designs. In 1930 he achieved his goal of winning a blue ribbon for his quilts from each of the 48 states.
Courtesy Philadelphia Inquirer

supplement, featured Emma and four of her quilts. She especially enjoyed the fan mail this publicity generated. Emma continued to make quilts until the care of her parents and full responsibility for the store absorbed all her free time. The cigar store gradually evolved into a museum for miniatures, and later, "Emma's Happiness Museum." On display were her quilts and other items she had acquired from her friends all over the country.

In some ways, the resurgence of quiltmaking in the 1970s and 1980s mirrored the quilt revival of the 1930s, and interest was focused on quilters of the earlier era. Emma's scrapbooks were the source for several articles on the quilt authorities who had been her correspondents.

National attention was again focused on Emma Andres and her quilts when they were featured in several national quilt magazines in the 1980s. In 1984, Emma won the Quilt Artisan Award and the Central Arizona Historical Society held an exhibit of her quilts in Phoenix.

All this prompted the Sharlot Hall Museum in Prescott to mount a display of Emma's quilts. She spent almost every day of the last three years of her life giving talks about her quilts and regaling visitors with quilting stories.

Arizona quilt artisans like Emma Andres, Rose Livingston, and Nellie Smith used their needlework to take quiltmaking into the realm of art. They followed a grand tradition of needle artisans before them, and they forged a trail for later artisans to follow.

Whether as a practical craft or as an art, quiltmaking follows grand traditions. The people of Arizona represents a rich diversity, so too the quilts and quiltmakers of Arizona reflect a diversity of origins and traditions. Many of these quilts, like their owners, have been transplanted to Arizona. Some came when Arizona was still a territory, some came quite recently. Through these quilts, we can trace the history and tradition of quiltmaking.

Robert Parker Family.

Courtesy Arizona Historical Society Library

Detail of Princess Feather quilt by Anna Mary Hoffman Fetter (1844–1921).
Courtesy Margaret Wilheim Francis

GRAND TRADITIONS

Tracing The History Of Quiltmaking

Detail, Baltimore Album quilt. Ruched roses were mixed with flowers with gathered petals, in a ruched vase. Ruching involved stitching, then gathering, a narrow folded fabric strip. This was arranged into a series of circles, forming a flower or other designs.

Courtesy Private Collection

First in horse-drawn wagons, and later in cars and planes, quilts have been brought to Arizona from all parts of the country. For those first settlers, quilts were part of their essential provisions. For those retiring in Arizona a century later, quilts are a piece of the home they left behind. As cherished heirlooms, family keepsakes, or simply as practical bedding, thousands of quilts have been transplanted to Arizona. Some were stitched in the comfort of fine homes in bustling cities, when Arizona was only Indian villages and Spanish pueblos. Many more were sewn in the first decades of this century.

Some of the quilts brought to Arizona are veritable treasures. With colors still bright, they are quilts of exceptional beauty or rarity. Even ordinary quilts may qualify as treasures; the value of a quilt is not only aesthetic but historical and sentimental. Spanning almost two centuries, and representing every region of the country, these quilts reflect the traditions of quiltmaking and, through them, we can trace the history of the craft.

CLASSICS FROM THE PAST

Among the earliest types of quilts were those of "whole cloth," or simply lengths of cloth seamed together. Throughout the eighteenth century, silk, cotton, or wool quilts, in rich colors and covered with fine quilting in elaborate designs, were highly prized in England and the American colonies. Some wool quilts were made from lustrous, glazed worsted cloth called calimanco.

A later and less fine example of this style is a whole-cloth wool quilt with a contrasting center square. Made in the early nineteenth century, the slightly coarse wool was reportedly hand-spun and hand-woven. The quilt's colors are the result of natural dyes.

With a heavy wool batt, the quilting stitches are necessarily large, approximately five per inch. The quilted spoked-wheel design in the center medallion is filled with diagonal lines. The rest of the quilt is covered with fan motifs, chevrons, waves, and triangles. The large buttonhole stitching in yarn on the edges of the quilt is a recent addition.

A cornucopia and flowers are outlined in white stitches on white fabric in a style known, appropriately enough, as "white work." So popular were the different types of white work that women would turn their colorful pieced or appliquéd quilts face down so that the plain white backings and the tracery of stitches were displayed. This elegantly quilted and stuffed pillow or table cover was made circa 1850, near the end of the period of popularity for this type of needlework.

The beautiful designs on this small piece are brought into high relief by stuffing or cording parts of each motif. This was usually done by separating the threads of the backing and inserting small tufts of batting material; loosely woven backing made this an easier task. This piece has such a backing, which could indicate it was hand-woven. In other instances the backing was slit then sewn closed after stuffing, but this method was not considered as desirable.

Further definition was given to the stuffed areas by closely quilting the background, which often gave the piece a stippled effect. This piece is unusual in that the only filling is in the padded areas and there is no background quilting. French

Whole Cloth Wool quilt, maker unknown, c.1840; pieced and quilted wool, 75" x 80."
Collection of Willcox Chamber of Commerce, Rex Allen Museum, Arizona

knots add embellishment and realism; the tops of the acorn motifs are studded with knots. Using a backstitch instead of the running stitch normally used in quilting, the maker was able to achieve an astonishing seventeen stitches per inch.

Medallion quilts, those with a central motif surrounded by a border or series of borders, echoed the design of white-work quilts. Early examples of pieced medallion-style quilts, dating from the end of the eighteenth century, usually featured simple patchwork and large pieces. After the turn of the century, designs became more intricate.

Small triangles, arranged into the Flying Geese pattern, frame the simple embroidered and appliquéd blocks on the linen-and-cotton Medallion quilt. Hearts and diamonds were appliquéd on a fabric inexplicably streaked with blue for five of the blocks and the wide borders. Four more linen blocks were decorated with crewel embroidery. Two of these were signed, using the tiny cross-stitch once learned by young girls for the purpose of "marking," or initialing and numbering, their future household linens:

Eliza Smith Goltho AD 1831 Age 11 Amen
Eliza Smith Mendon AD 1832 Age 12 Amen

The quilting, in zigzag lines, is not particularly small or fine; that characteristic, and the simplicity of the appliqué shapes, lead one to assume that the entire quilt was the work of young Miss Eliza Smith.

Two quilts, also in the medallion style, represent the quilters' fascination with the beautiful and colorful fabric known as chintz. The fabric of fashion in the eighteenth century, chintz was made in India by the painstaking method of handbrushing the dyes and mordants. (Some natural dyes would color fabric directly; others required a mordant, a substance used to fix the coloring matter, such as nitrate of iron, to make the fibers absorb the dyes.) In floral or arborescent designs, the fabrics were usually glazed, which gave a sheen to the rich colors. Quilted bedcoverings of chintz, called palampores, were highly prized.

In America, chintz was both imported and produced. Since the fabric was frequently hard to obtain and always expensive, the printed motifs were sometimes cut from sewing scraps or from a yard or two purchased for this purpose and appliquéd to another piece of fabric. So popular was this style that fabric manufacturers began to print motifs expressly for quilts, such as panels with birds, urns, or baskets.

White Work quilt, maker unknown,
Pennsylvania, c. 1850; quilted and
stuffed cotton, 22" x 38."
Courtesy Ann Clare

Medallion quilt by Eliza Smith, 1832;
pieced and appliquéd cotton and linen
with embroidery, 87" x 88."
Courtesy Lilla J. Krautbaurer

*Broderie Perse quilt, maker unknown,
Georgia, c. 1825; appliquéd chintz,
105" x 108."*
Courtesy Marjorie Buell Richards

This technique, called Broderie Perse ("Persian embroidery"), was used in both quilts shown here. Although some quilts did contain embroidery for details or embellishment, the term actually refers to the Persian practice of embroidering on a fragile fabric, then cutting and appliquéing the piece onto a sturdier cloth. *The Dictionary of Needlework*, published in 1882, describes the Broderie Perse method: "Stretch the background upon a frame...and paste the chintz flowers into position upon it. When the pasting is finished and dry, take the work out of the frame and stitch loosely with as little visibility as possible, all around the leaves and flowers." A buttonhole stitch was sometimes used, as well as the conventional whipstitch.

Women in eastern seaboard cities had the greatest access to chintz fabrics; the Broderie Perse style of quilt was especially popular in the South, where many women could afford such expensive goods and had sufficient free time to devote the many hours necessary for such stitchery.

The Broderie Perse quilt shown, which is made in the framed medallion style, is possibly one such quilt. It was taken from a home in Georgia by James Bull, a Union soldier under General William Tecumseh Sherman, who took part in the destructive "March to the Sea" during the Civil War; the quilt-maker is unknown. Bull, a member of Company F of the Illinois Volunteer Army, was one of the sixty thousand men who cut a forty-mile-wide swath between Atlanta and Savannah, severing the Confederate Army's supply lines and hastening the end of the war. Many homes were burned and their contents acquired as the spoils of war. Bull, who had served in the siege of Vicksburg the year before, removed the quilt from its home somewhere in Georgia. After Bull was discharged from the Union Army in 1865, he returned to his home in Illinois, bringing the Broderie Perse quilt with him. It was eventually passed to his great-granddaughter, who brought the quilt to Arizona.

Beautifully balanced, with intricate floral shapes complementing the fabric borders, the quilt was closely quilted in a diagonal grid. The Tree of Life design, the most popular design in printed palampores, was adapted to a smaller scale on the sides of this quilt. Some of the motifs, such as the pheasant and basket, are found on several other Broderie Perse quilts dating from the late eighteenth and early nineteenth centuries. Since each quilt is very different in the final arrangement of the pieces, the creativity and ingenuity of the American quiltmaker is demonstrated as well.

ABOVE: Anna Maria Livingston Rutgers.
Courtesy Louise Crafts

LEFT: Broderie Perse quilt by Anna Maria Livingston Rutgers (1817–1886), New Jersey, c. 1850; appliquéd chintz, 94" x 94."
Courtesy Louise Crafts

Also in the medallion style, but with an open lacy effect, is the Broderie Perse top made by Anna Maria Livingston Rutgers. The background was constructed in sections, the floral motifs arranged to disguise the seams. The intricate shapes, including spindly leaves and stems as narrow as an eighth of an inch, are attached with minute stitches, in a light-colored, very fine thread. The top was signed in ink in a corner on the back: "A.M. Rutgers." Interestingly, the signature would be completely hidden if the quilt had been finished.

Anna Maria Livingston, born in 1817, married John Livingston Rutgers in 1843. Both were from prominent New Jersey families: the first governor of New Jersey was a Livingston and the Rutgers family founded Rutgers University. The quilt top was handed down through the family to Anna's grand-daughter, Luna Rutgers Morgan. Having no children of her own, she gave the quilt to the present owner, a family friend.

Toward the middle of the nineteenth century, women began to make their quilts in a repeated block format instead of the medallion style. Both pieced and appliquéd quilts were made block by block, which were easier to handle than the large pieces of the earlier style. Made in approximately 1860, this quilt has nine identical appliqué blocks surrounded by a curving vine with leaves.

Appliqué, from the French *appliquer*, or "to lay down,"

involves sewing shapes to background after first turning under a seam allowance. Unfinished examples exist that show the techniques used in attaching the shapes. Usually they were basted in place, then the seam allowances were tucked under with the needle as they were sewn. (Some early pieces have been found with the edges first basted under.) The stitching was usually done in white thread, with no effort made to match the piece. A small whipstitch or less commonly, the buttonhole stitch, was used.

Most appliqué designs were representational, with floral motifs most common. Perhaps original, this design includes a stylized flower with fleur-de-lis motifs instead of buds. The appliqué border, with the vine smoothly turning each corner, reflects careful planning. Quilted feathered wreaths, surrounded by lines of quilting less than half an inch apart, are done with extremely even and tiny stitches. The color combination of red and green accented with gold was very fashionable for patch-work as well as appliqué in the 1800s.

Solomon's Crown, the name given the quilt by the maker's family, was made by a lady known only as Mrs. Judd, the step-mother of the present owner's grandmother. Made in Indiana, the quilt travelled to Iowa and Nebraska before being brought to Arizona. (More than a hundred years after its creation, the quilt is displayed in the owner's home and enjoyed daily.)

Solomon's Crown quilt by Mrs. Judd,
Indiana, c. 1860; appliquéd cotton,
88" x 96."
Courtesy Mary Karsk

One of the most charming traditions connected with quilt-making is that of bridal quilts. Young girls prepared for marriage by making several tops, usually waiting until the engagement was announced to quilt them. At that time, another quilt would be started, a special one, finer in both fabric and technique. Bridal quilts were usually the best or most ornate a woman would ever make.

Traditionally, thirteen quilts were required, twelve "regular" and one bridal. Most women would have felt extremely fortunate to have had so many, however. Bethenia Owen-Adair, who was sixteen when she married in 1854, wrote: "During the winter and early spring, I put in all my spare time in preparing for my approaching marriage. I had four quilts already pieced, ready for the lining; mother had given me the lining for them all, and the cotton for two, and we quilted and finished them all....In addition, mother gave me a good feather bed, and pillows, a good straw bed, a pair of blankets and two extra quilts....I had high hopes and great expectations for the future." A nineteenth-century Canadian family with nine daughters also vigorously upheld this tradition. Only one daughter married, and after the death of the last surviving sister, one hundred and fifteen unused quilts were found in trunks in the family home.

Many of the quilts known as bridal quilts were appliquéd rather than pieced, probably due to the desire to incorporate the romantic imagery of hearts and flowers. Other reasons for appliqué being saved for special quilts are practical ones; the added expense of large pieces of cloth for the background, as well as the amount of time expended, was too great for quilts meant for everyday use.

Among the many fabric flowers that were coaxed into bloom with a needle, none was more favored by quilters than the rose. The Rose of Sharon pattern had obvious romantic connotations and was a popular design for bride's quilts. Even when the designs were not floral, they showcased the quilt-maker's skills.

Anna Mary Hoffman Felter, when making the quilt for her dower chest, chose the large, swirling design of the Princess Feather. The design, also known as Prince's Feather, is based on the feathery plumes used as the symbol of the Prince of Wales. The curves on the edges of each plume make this pattern a challenge to even the most accomplished quilter. Amazingly, Anna Mary chose to do some of this intricate appliqué by machine.

This Princess Feather quilt shows a combination of hand

ABOVE: Anna Mary Hoffman Felter, maker of the Princess Feather quilt. Using the sewing machine for some of the appliqué, Anna Mary made the quilt during the Civil War as part of her dower chest.

LEFT: Princess Feather quilt by Anna Mary Hoffman Felter (1844–1921), Pennsylvania, 1865; appliquéd cottons, 87" x 90."

Courtesy Margaret Wilhelm Francis

and machine work. One large motif is centered in the quilt, with similar shapes forming a border. The spines of the feathers and the narrow ovals in the outer shapes are done in reverse appliqué, a technique where the top piece is cut and stitched to show another layer of fabric. Machine stitching was used on some long smooth curves, as well as on a few serrated edges. Even some of the tiny reverse-appliqué ovals are done on the machine. We can only guess at the reasoning behind the mixed techniques, since there is no pattern to the placement of the different stitching. Did the maker start by sewing the edges by machine, then revert to the more careful method of hand stitching? Or did she begin the project by hand and then decide to use the machine as her confidence in her new tool increased?

Anna Mary Hoffman Felter, born in Pennsylvania in 1844, only four years after her family emigrated from Austria, made the quilt during the Civil War years. She married Joseph Felter at the end of the war. The mother of five children, Anna Felter was known for her "folk medicine" and herbal cures. She rarely used the quilt, and her granddaughter, who brought the quilt to Arizona, has also saved the quilt for special occasions.

Certainly the most spectacular of appliqué quilts were the album quilts made in the mid-nineteenth century. So many were made in Baltimore, Maryland, that the city's name became

attached to this style. Album quilts reflected the popularity of the autograph album and featured blocks with inked or embroidered signatures of their contributors. Pieced album quilts almost always featured the same pattern throughout, made from various prints, usually with a plain center area for inscriptions. Appliqué album quilts could have a variety of different blocks. Lavish displays of needlework skills, patriotism, and artistic sensibilities, the multiple-block quilts were also made as bridal quilts and for presentation and commemorative purposes, and represent the apex of the album quilt style.

Today, Baltimore Album quilts are extremely rare and valuable, which added to the excitement when one such quilt was unfolded at the Quilt Documentation Day held in Prescott. Little history is available on this outstanding example, but the quilt itself offers tantalizing clues to its past. Similar quilts were made in Baltimore between 1846 and 1854 by a group of Methodist women and this particular example has many of the motifs found on those quilts. The wreaths of roses, vases of flowers, cornucopias, and spread-winged eagle are similar, if not identical, to elements found on these others. On closer inspection, one can see the small touches that make this quilt unique. The cornucopia block, second from the left on the fourth row, has faint pencil lines, indicating a change in the

placement of the pieces. The *èpergne* of fruit on the same row is complete with knife, as if ready to cut the plump apple or pear. Tiny ovals of black were once inked in the pink fabric center of the watermelon; they have long since deteriorated the fabric, and now the background peeks through. The quilt is somewhat different from most Baltimore Album quilts in the amount of quilting. Tiny, even stitches, in rows less than a quarter-inch apart, cover the quilt and create a stippled effect.

The arrangement of the blocks is pleasing and balanced; great care was obviously taken to place the wreaths and vases opposite similar blocks. The eagle, in vivid blue fondu, or shaded fabric, provides a focal point while pineapple blocks, visually heavier than the other blocks, anchor each corner. The curving vine is a final graceful frame.

The inscriptions in ink and cross-stitch suggest the makers' identities: "Sarah A. Culley 1846," "M. Murray 1846," "E. Evans," and the initials "M.A.H." are found on four of the blocks. The quilt was brought to Arizona by the present owner, who inherited it from her great-aunt, Edith Rush Price. "I have a quilt I need to tell you about," was all that was ever said of it; Edith Price died before revealing the origins of this spectacular piece.

In contrast, the record of the another exquisite Baltimore Album quilt is well known and entwined with the lives of its owners. Made in 1856, the quilt was "Presented to Rev. D. Kreamer by the ladies of the Emmanuel Church of Baltimore as a testimony of their affectionate regard." Each block was made and, it is believed, quilted by different churchwomen. Each also signed her block, signatures stamped or written in thread or ink.

As with many group-made quilts, the blocks vary in design and expertise. Simple designs are combined with the more ornate: primitive fruit shapes take their place alongside multi-layered roses. Appropriately, bibles and a dove with olive branch are centered in three of the open floral wreaths. The flag and shield-bearing eagle are placed at the top, leaving the center block for the quilt's dedication. Sashing was cut from a lovely red paisley print, and an ornate striped fabric provided the border.

ABOVE: Detail, Baltimore Album quilt. Flowers in wreath were padded for a realistic effect. Inscription reads "M. Murray 1846."

RIGHT: Baltimore Album quilt, maker unknown, Maryland, 1846; appliquéd cottons, 102" x 101."
Private collection

PREVIOUS PAGE: Appliquéd eagle demonstrates careful use of "fondu" printed fabric. Printed rings were used for claws and corners of shield.

ABOVE: Detail, Baltimore Album quilt.
Woven basket illustrates a creative use of
fabrics; wavy design on yellow fabric help
form realistic bird and basket rim and
handles.

LEFT: Baltimore Album quilt, Ladies of the
Emanuel Church, Maryland, 1856;
appliquéd cottons, 101" x 100."
Private collection

Daniel Kreamer, the recipient of this glorious quilt, was born in Pennsylvania in 1825 and entered the ministry of the Evangelical Association when he came of age. After serving the congregation in Baltimore for six years, he was transferred to Illinois. According to a tribute written upon the Reverend Kreamer's death in 1906, the years spent in Baltimore "...were years of great joy and scores of souls were saved." Passed from father to son for four generations, the quilt came to Arizona with its present owner, the great-grandson of Daniel Kreamer. An enduring tribute to its recipient, the quilt's bouquets of appreciation still bloom.

PICTURED IN PATCHWORK

Hundreds, or perhaps thousands, of patchwork patterns are based on a handful of geometric shapes: the square, the circle, the diamond, the hexagon, and various types of triangles. Using these basic shapes, a quilter could create a stylized, geometric version of the world around her. Taking inspiration from everyday surroundings, she could recreate in fabric the pattern of flying geese against the sunset, or mountain ranges in the distance, or stars in the night sky.

Until the late 1800s, which saw the publication of quilt patterns in newspapers and ladies' magazines, most designs were passed or traded among family and friends, copied from other quilts, or were original to that quiltmaker. There was little emphasis on pattern names until the publishing of patterns became prevalent. Then, names were taken from literature, politics, and events. The Bible was also a rich source for descriptive names; Rose of Sharon, King David's Crown, Star of Bethlehem, to name but a few.

One of the oldest and most beloved of all quilt patterns is the star. Most familiar is the large eight-pointed Star of Bethlehem or Lone Star, composed of hundreds of variegated diamonds. A simpler variation, made with squares and triangles, is the Variable Star. A superb sampler of the red prints then available, the Variable Star quilt shows the graphic beauty of this simple design.

Warm red prints such as those used in this quilt were called madder-red, or in the "madder style." The dye was originally obtained from madder root, which was later replaced with the aniline dye of alizarin red; a rich chocolate brown was also obtained from madder dye. Reds were popular with quilters of the past because of their fastness, or ability to hold the original color, a trait that allows these stars to shine forth almost a century and a half later.

While many of the red prints in this piece show wear, the

Variable Star quilt, maker unknown, c. 1850;

pieced cotton and chintz, 97" x 98."

Collecton of Edward C. Flagg

chintz setting fabric has its original sheen. It is likely that the stars were cut from used pieces of cloth, while the chintz was new. Perhaps the fabric was saved for years before being put to lovely use in the mid-century quilt. Sprigged designs such is this were called floral-trail prints and were produced very early in the nineteenth century.

The quilt is part of the impressive collection of Mary Harkness White Flagg. The Flaggs came to Arizona in 1914 when Mary's husband Arthur accepted the position of superintendent of the Sultana Copper Mine in Kelvin. The family purchased the quilts during summer excursions to New England and at auctions at storage facilities in Phoenix.

Nine glorious stars, made from a beautiful array of prints and patterns, are punctuated with small red stars in this variation of the Star of Bethlehem. Set edge-to-edge, hence the name Touching Stars, all the stars are made of chintz and roller-printed fabrics.

Roller-printing, which began in the early 1800s, revolutionized the textile industry. The ancient method of block printing and the newer technique of copperplate printing were both overshadowed by this accelerated method, in which engraved copper rollers were inked from color troughs as the fabric rolled through in a continuous strip. During the same years, experi-

mentation with mineral dyes resulted in a new palette of colors, somewhat harsher than those created with vegetable dyes.

Each of the stars contains a wonderful assortment of fabrics. Two have fabric motifs perfectly centered in some of the diamonds, which required extra care in cutting as well as extra fabric. A vibrant red print was used for the accent stars and the simple yet effective border. Softly complementing the patchwork were quilted "feathers," plume-like shapes arranged in circles or curving lines. The quilt was purchased in Pennsylvania by an Arizona antique dealer.

Feathered Star quilt patterns have long been considered a test of a quiltmaker's skills; the shapes are simple enough, but the small size of the pieces and the difficulty in planning their placement have earned the pattern this reputation.

Perfectly symmetrical, each of the stars on this particular Feathered Star quilt was centered with a patchwork sunburst. The sawtooth edges create a wonderful twinkling effect. The addition of pink-and-green sashing between the blocks was a bold graphic touch. The unusual appliqué border motifs resemble holly leaves; the green shows some color changes, not uncommon considering the unreliability of that color. Since no single vegetable dye would produce the color green, it was obtained by overdying yellow with blue.

146

Touching Stars quilt, maker unknown, Pennsylvania, c. 1860; pieced cotton and chintz, 111" x 113."

Collection of William W. Pilcher

Feathered Stars quilt, maker unknown,
Missouri, c. 1870; pieced and appliquéd
cotton, 69" x 89."
Courtesy Jackie Ellsworth Bronander

Feathered Stars with Maze quilt by Lottie Belle Meyers Gebhart Bisbee (1873–1962), Indiana, c. 1900; pieced cotton, 62" x 81."

Courtesy Mary L. and Harold G. Adelfson

The different fastness capacity of the two colors resulted in quilts with bluish or yellowish greens, or spots of either color. A synthetic green dye, introduced in 1875, also gave mixed results; instead of fading to a lighter green, the dyed fabrics often faded to light tan color. (Many beautiful old quilts have vivid red and strong yellow mixed with pale tan—color choices that would be perplexing if one was not aware that the tan was probably once a rich, dark green.)

This quilt was purchased in Missouri in 1889 by the family of the current owner; it was one of three bought from two sisters, at three dollars each, to replace bedding lost in a house fire. The sisters' names are not known, but their handiwork is dated 1870; a subsequent owner added another name and date.

Blue and white was another color combination much favored by nineteenth-century quiltmakers. Indigo blue fabrics were reliable, colorfast, and offered sharp contrast to the background muslin, resulting in quilts with unparalleled graphic qualities.

The blue fabric in the Feathered Star with Maze appears as a solid, but actually is figured with tiny white diamonds. This fabric was used for the small, three-quarter-inch triangles that edge each star and the unusual appliquéd circles dotting each block. Both appliqué and piecing were stitched entirely by hand. The blocks are divided by a Garden Maze sashing, which appears overly large and heavy because of the delicacy of the stars. The quilting is all grids and diagonal lines less than an inch apart, done in small, very even stitches.

The quilt was made by Lottie Belle Meyer Gebhart Bisbee in Indiana around the turn of the century. Little is known about her life other than some prominent dates; born in 1873 and widowed for the first time in 1905, she came to Winslow, Arizona, in 1912 with her son, and married again. She lived in Winslow until her death at the age of eighty-eight. Family friends were given this and other quilts following the death of her son.

Four large, vibrant stars made up of triangles cover the surface of an unusual quilt from the 1870s. In turkey red, antimony orange, and teal blue, the triangles were combined with a light fabric for an interesting and original design. (Color changes on some of the blue triangles are an indication that those pieces may once have been green.)

To achieve the pinwheel effect, each of the identical stars was given a quarter turn before they were joined. The yellow forms a complete inner border, while the red and teal edge two sides each on the outer border. The only quilting was in simple diagonal lines.

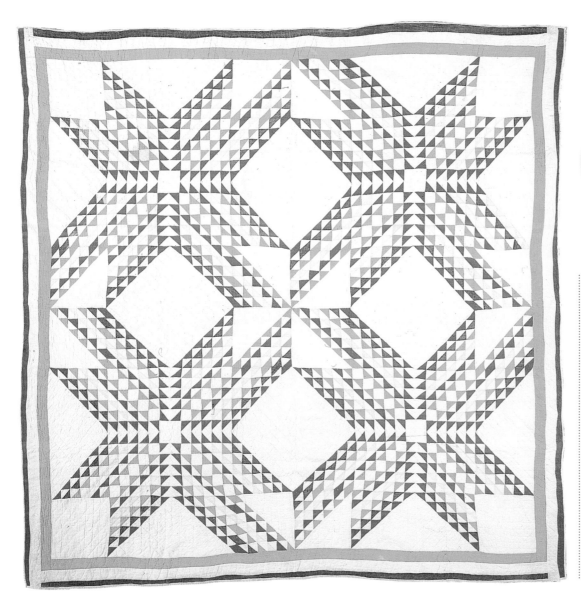

ABOVE: Katherine Hook Lathan Beagle (left) with daughter Nettie Hauser. Katherine Beagle, maker of the Pinwheel Star quilt, was spry and agile into her nineties. She could outrun her 7-year-old great-grandson, who is now the proud owner of the quilt.

LEFT: Pinwheel Star quilt by Katherine S. Hook Lathan Beagle (1840–1930), Ohio, c. 1865; pieced cotton, 78" x 78."
Courtesy Don W. Smith

Katherine Hook Lathan Beagle, the quiltmaker, lived her entire life in Ohio. Born in 1840, she was the mother of five and was widowed twice. She followed the antebellum practice of protecting the skin, and never left the house without gloves and a wide-brimmed hat. Her great-grandson, the present owner of the quilt, remembers that Katherine always walked "straight as a stick" and wouldn't tolerate bad posture in anyone around her. He also recalls that she was kind and generous and was considered by all as "a pleasure to know."

In vibrant colors and bold design, the Eight-Pointed Star quilt is representative of a people and their unique way of life. From Switzerland and Germany, the Amish and Mennonite sects settled first in Pennsylvania and lived strict yet simple rural lives. Guided by biblical passages such as "Be ye not conformed to this world..." (Romans 12:2), they adopted simple dress in solid colors; even today, the Amish travel by horse and buggy and have lantern-lit homes. The Mennonites are less strict, however, and some use modern conveniences and wear regular dress.

Old Amish and Mennonite quilts are distinctive because they were pieced using solid colors only. Made of wool or cotton, the quilts generally displayed simple patchwork designs, such as Bars or Diamond in a Square, although sometimes the more detailed Sunshine and Shadow or Nine Patch patterns were beautifully executed, with a juxtaposition of colors and intricate quilting.

The Eight-Pointed Star, made by Katie Reiner Hepler, a Pennsylvania German Mennonite, has these qualities. The gold and red may seem too bright to have been used for clothing, but such colors, combined with black, make the quilts and clothing of the Amish and Mennonites distinctive. Quilted concentric circles fill the star; the background triangles are covered in a grid of small stitches. A large seven-strand cable is quilted in the border, beautifully framing the piece. The date, 1901, is carefully embroidered in a place of honor on the gold border.

A circle with radiating points is a common design in most cultures and was frequently used as a quilt pattern. Some of these patterns resemble stars, sunbursts, or sunflowers, but when there are thirty-two points, as on a navigational chart, we can assume the inspiration was a mariner's compass.

Even before the magnetic compass was discovered in the thirteenth century, sailors in the Mediterranean used the eight predictable winds to navigate. These were represented on sea charts by a design called a "wind rose." When the magnetic compass became common, this same design was used to signify the four directions. Quiltmakers with access to maps would

Eight-Pointed Star quilt by Katie Reiner
Hepler, Pennsylvania, 1901; pieced cotton,
81" x 82."
Collection of Audrey Collins Waite

surely have been intrigued by the possibilities of the compass design, and quilts made in this pattern date from as early as the first quarter of the nineteenth century.

This particular example was made in approximately 1860, and little advance planning seems to have been done before the appliqué began. The red fabric has been precisely pieced into thirty-two points; the orientation is slightly skewed; the four longest points should be vertical and horizontal. The misdirection is probably due to the method used to construct the quilt: instead of cutting the background fabric into squares, it was left as one large piece, and the compasses were then appliquéd in place and the fabric behind them trimmed later.

A sinuous vine with flowers decorates the borders. The green fabric was originally a print, but much of the figuring has disintegrated due to iron in the black dye, leaving tiny areas of the figures threadbare. Two of the flowers are heavily stuffed, one by inserting cotton through the threads of the backing fabric, the other through a small cut made in the backing. Either the maker was unsatisfied with the results or found both methods too tedious to continue.

The maker obviously enjoyed the quilting process, however; feather circles decorate the plain areas and a running feather follows the vine in the border. The background areas are covered in a tiny grid. All the quilting was done with exquisitely tiny stitches.

The quiltmaker, known only as Mrs. Maffett, lived in Tennessee. The quilt was given to her great-granddaughter, who in turn gave it to a friend. The embroidered date in one corner, 1736, was added later and probably represents an incorrect conjecture of when the quilt was made.

The only clue to the identity of the maker of this striking red-and-white quilt was the note found pinned to it: "Made by Aunt Minnie in Indiana." The quilt was purchased at the Goodwill Industries Antique Sale held annually in Phoenix and was donated by the family of the quiltmaker.

Dating from the end of the 1800s, the quilt was hand-pieced in the Delectable Mountains pattern, which was named for the beautiful range of mountains described in John Bunyan's 1678 allegorical tale, *Pilgrim's Progress.* The design was frequently made by quilters, but most of whom ensured that all the triangles pointed towards each corner, making a symmetrical design. "Aunt Minnie" perhaps preferred a more individualistic approach.

Beginning about 1840, red and white was a favored color scheme for quilts. The reliability of turkey-red cotton fabrics, both printed and plain, certainly contributed to this popularity.

Delectable Mountains quilt by "Aunt Minnie", Indiana, c. 1890; pieced cotton, 77" x 78."
Collection of Helen King

Turkey-red, named for the country of origin, was a dyeing process, not an actual dye. The turkey-red fabric in the Delectable Mountains quilt appears to be a solid color but actually has small white dots about every inch. The quilt has a simple quilting design of an allover grid.

While many quilt patterns were obviously representational, a secondary or abstract design was sometimes created when several blocks were combined. Known as "Pine Tree" by the family, this quilt design gives the illusion of curves even though every edge is really straight. The quilt has wonderful visual movement, due no doubt to the fact that the intersections of the blocks resemble spinning windmill blades.

Two different green prints are used in the quilt: yellow and white ovals dot the fabric used for the "trees," while a floral was used for the triangles of the Flying Geese in the border. The quilting is basic, mostly straight lines and grids, but the stitches are exceptionally small and even.

Made in Missouri by Margaret Gibson Ballew, the quilt was an 1896 wedding gift to one of her six children. Margaret, who had eloped at sixteen to escape the control of a harsh stepfather, knitted, tatted, and wove rugs on a carpet loom in addition to making quilts. This piece is a treasured possession of Margaret Ballew's great-grandson.

Wild Goose Chase is another pattern that becomes more dynamic when many blocks are joined. Based on the simple triangle unit of the Flying Geese quilt pattern, the Wild Goose Chase design crosses each block diagonally, creating movement and interest.

The amount of quilting reflects the need to secure the cotton batting adequately. Whether homemade or commercial, cotton battings tended to shift or separate unless they were held in place by numerous rows of stitching. In this case, lines only one half-inch apart completely cover the background. A feathered wreath design accents the plain areas.

The quiltmaker, known only as Mrs. Winkle, gave the quilt as a gift to her neighbor in Iowa, the current owner's mother-in-law.

"WASTE NOT, WANT NOT"

The scrapbag, bulging with bits of cloth left over from the family's sewing or good sections cut from outgrown clothing, was the source for many wonderful, and appropriately named, scrap quilts. Perhaps this was the only fabric available for quiltmaking, or perhaps the quiltmaker merely wanted to put the pieces of fabric to good use. In the late 1800s, women even used the scraps from finer fabrics, including silks and velvets,

Pine Burr quilt (called Pine Tree by family) by Margaret Gibson Ballew, Missouri, 1896; pieced cotton, 68" x 82."

Courtesy Donald Hoff

resulting in quilts that were a curious mix of economy and extravagance. Anyone who has done the hard work of hand-spinning or hand-weaving would hesitate to discard good cotton cloth. The habit of not wasting anything—food or fabric—was deeply ingrained in women of the past.

It is also likely that women simply felt challenged by the diversity of color and pattern the scraps presented. It was a challenge to make a quilt when a piece of fabric would not yield the necessary number of patches, a lesson in color to make the design appear uniform while using a variety of fabrics. It was interesting, and probably fun, too, to combine as many prints as possible in a single quilt. There was even a fad for "charm quilts," ones where every single patch was a different fabric.

The fact that quiltmakers of the past incorporated used fabric in their quilts, as shown by the quilts and the stories of the women that made them, is evidence of remarkable resourcefulness. Although it is unlikely that worn fabric would be used in a special quilt, one with an intricate pattern or elaborate quilting, it is possible that such cloth would be part of one meant for daily use. The cloth would have to have been in relatively good condition though, since quiltmakers would not willingly compromise the durability of their project at the outset.

The Single Irish Chain quilt, made of Nine Patch blocks alternating with plain squares, appears to have just one patterned fabric throughout, but in various stages of fading and wear. The fabric, printed with the tiny white stars that were seen on many fabrics around the nation's Centennial, was originally a rich navy blue. In some blocks—both pieced and plain—it appears in the dark shade; other squares are a medium blue, and some are an extremely faded gray-blue. The remarkable thing about this is the amount of wear on some of the pieces: the lighter the color, the more use is evident. This wear had obviously take place before the quilt was made, as practically new pieces are adjacent to the fraying, worn ones. Some loose stitching reveals that the seam allowances of the lightest squares were once darker. Perhaps when the quilt was made the various pieces were closer in color, even though some had seen different amounts of use.

The resulting pattern shows the versatility of a simple block like the Nine Patch. The blocks of gray and white stand out as distinct blocks, while the blocks with the darker blue blend with the background, leaving the white squares to form the links in the chain that gives this pattern its name.

The quiltmaker, Susan Wise Moses, had also seen and survived many hardships. Married to Jacob Moses in 1848, she was

Wild Goose Chase quilt (called Flying Geese by family) by Mrs. Winkle, Iowa, c. 1910; pieced cotton, 65" x 78."

Courtesy Jane Ann Juel

the mother of three when a fire destroyed the family home and business, an inn in Pennsylvania. Making a new start in Ohio, they had five more children, one of whom died in infancy. Their sixth child was Phoebe Anne Moses, who later became famous as Annie Oakley, the sharpshooter.

When Jacob died in 1866, Susan was forced to work as a nurse. The younger children were often left in the care of their older sister, and on one of these occasions, Annie used her father's "Old Kentucky" rifle to shoot a squirrel. A neighbor, Dan Brumbaugh, who often brought meat and produce to the

struggling family, heard about the squirrel, and offered Annie shooting lessons. Susan married him in 1867, a few months after the death of her oldest daughter. The family moved to the Brumbaugh home and, two years later, Susan gave birth to another daughter. Heartbreak again followed happiness when her husband had a fatal accident later that year. Susan later married a widower named

Shaw. Annie supplemented the family income by shooting and selling game to a hotel in Cincinnati.

While living in Cincinnati in 1875, Annie was encouraged by the hotel owner to accept the challenge of a shooting match against Frank Butler, a renowned marksman. He would later recall "...never did a person make more impossible shots than that little girl." Annie, then only fifteen, won both the match and the heart of Frank Butler. With the one hundred dollar prize money, she purchased gifts for her family, including dress goods for her sisters and mother. A year later, she married Frank Butler and eventually became his partner. The better part of her career was spent with the Wild West show of William F. (Buffalo Bill) Cody.

Susan was a meticulous seamstress and taught all her daughters to sew by making quilts, and her oldest daughters were able to help support the family during some of the hard times by doing sewing. Annie used these skills in making her costumes and always travelled with her sewing machine. Contrary to the way plays and motion pictures have presented her, Annie Oakley made her costumes from broadcloth not buckskin. Sewn by Annie and two of her sisters, the costumes had to be washable and were made short and full to enable Annie to do trick horseback riding and other stunts.

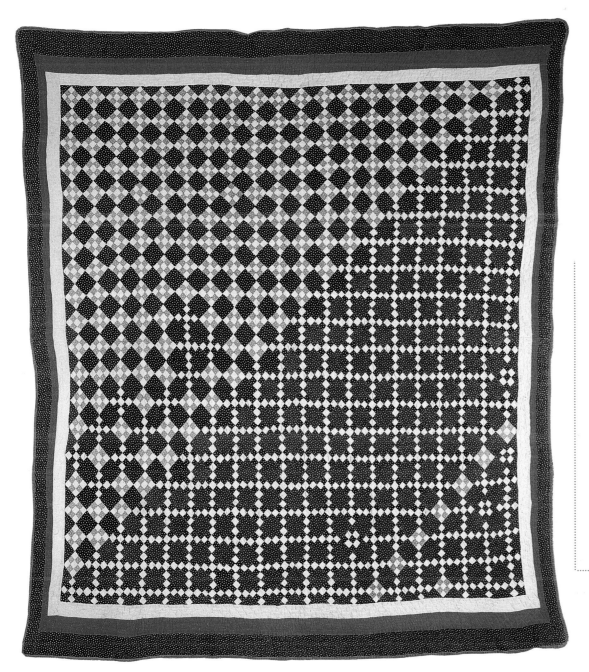

ABOVE: *Susan Wise Moses, maker of the Single Irish Chain quilt, was a Quaker and the mother of 9 children, one of whom gained fame as Annie Oakley.*
Courtesy Garst Museum, Greenville, Ohio

LEFT: *Single Irish Chain quilt by Susan Wise Moses (1832–1908), Ohio, c. 1880; pieced cotton, 68" x 88."*
Courtesy Betty Pickart

OPPOSITE: *Annie Oakley (Phoebe Anne Moses Butler) in costume. Annie made her own show outfits, she was taught to sew by piecing quilts.*

Susan Moses's quilt, patriotic in look, with the white stars on blue-and-red stripes in the border, was simply, and perhaps hurriedly, quilted in an overlapping fan design. It is owned by Susan Moses's great-great-granddaughter.

When Ruth Perkins was married in 1920, her wedding present from her aunt, Annette Wood, was a remarkable quilt top. Annette Wood lived near McLean, New York, and was known to have clairvoyant powers. Ruth Perkins remembered visiting her aunt as a child and recalled the horses and buggies lined up on the dirt road to her aunt's house, which was filled with people there to beseech Annette Wood to use her abilities to communicate with the dead or to find lost children.

Constructed of nearly five thousand pieces, the quilt's name stems from the fact that the one-inch squares used were just about the size of a postage stamp. A wonderful sampling of a wide variety of prints, most of which date to the turn of the century, the quilt top was probably pieced much earlier than the wedding year, since the maker was quite elderly at the time she gave it to Mrs. Perkins. However, as it was not uncommon for fabrics to remain in a family's scrapbag for decades before being used, an exact date is difficult to determine.

Some seams are more ridged than others, indicating that at least some of the squares were joined in five-patch sections before being added to the quilt. Some kind of order was

derived—intentionally or accidentally—by having most of the red and pink squares arranged in a X design across the surface. The pink squares provide a vivid sampling of the hundreds of prints of this color and scale; here two shades of pink in small floral or vermicular designs were printed on a white background. Upon receiving the quilt top, Ruth Perkins paid a church group to quilt it in a simple diagonal grid. Now owned by her daughter, the quilt is regarded as a precious heirloom.

Corn and Beans, the charming name of the pattern of a marvelous scrap quilt, was one of many patterns presented by the Ladies Art Company in 1889. Their catalog, "Diagrams of Quilt, Sofa and Pincushion Patterns," included three hundred designs; each pattern sold for a dime. For many patterns, this catalog provides the earliest documentation of names, but a number of designs are labeled only "A Simple Design" and "Sawtooth Patchwork."

Made by Alice Simpson McNeill Putnam, the grandmother of the present owner, the Corn and Beans quilt is a wonderful collection of late nineteenth-century prints. Plaids, stripes, paisleys, and dots were combined with florals in large and small triangles that form the design; even the backing is pieced from several different fabrics. A red-and-white stripe binds the edges of the all-over fan-quilted piece.

The Putnams owned a general merchandise store in Iowa

Postage Stamp quilt by Annette Wood, New York; c. 1920, pieced cotton, 70" x 70."

Courtesy Shirley R. Houk

that stocked groceries, appliances, rugs, and of course, fabrics. Alfred Putnam was also the inventor of a measuring device for fabric. Without knowing the family history, it might be assumed that the scrap look of this quilt was the result of extreme economy. Instead, it appears that the variety of fabrics was a deliberate matter of choice, not circumstance.

Another scrap quilt contains the same wide spectrum of prints, but in colors and designs of the 1930s. All sorts of prints are used for the diamonds of the little four-inch stars, and solids are used for the background. The overall effect, especially when viewed from a distance, is impressionistic; parts of the pattern seem to disappear, while the eye is drawn to other areas of high contrast.

Improved printing capabilities resulted in prints with more detail and colors than before. The lighter, clearer colors that began appearing in the mid-twenties must have been a refreshing change from the usual dark calicoes. One particular color is especially associated with the Depression years. A grayed-green, known as "Thirties green" by many of today's quilters, was called "nile green" in the 1927 Sears, Roebuck & Company catalog; squares of this color are scattered across the surface of the Stars quilt.

Nannie Catherine Buie Bunkley Crabb made a Stars quilt in Texas in the late 1930s, using scraps from other quilts and dressmaking material. Born in Alabama in 1872, she moved with her family to West Texas when she was eleven. Five years later, Nannie's family moved to another location in Texas, cutting short her romance with Thomas Crabb. She later married Thomas Nelson Bunkley, a doctor, and settled in Stamford, Texas.

As busy as she was with four children and a large house to maintain, Nannie found time for needlework; she also pursued an interest in photography and had her own darkroom. In 1917, her life was completely changed by the death of her

husband. Forced to give up her spacious home, Nannie used her sewing skills for income. Almost twenty years later, she rekindled her romance with Thomas Crabb, her girlhood beau, who had married, raised a family, and been widowed in the interim. The sweetheart ring

ABOVE: Alice Simpson McNeill Putnam, whose husband owned a general store, had a wide assortment of fabrics from which to choose for her quilt.
Courtesy Peggy H. Putnam

LEFT: Corn and Beans quilt by Alice Simpson McNeill Putnam (1888–1937), Iowa, c. 1870; pieced cotton, 75" x 84."
Courtesy Peggy H. Putnam

OPPOSITE: Texas home of Nannie Catherine Buie Bunkley Crabb, maker of the Stars quilt. The family was forced to sell the home at the death of her first husband.
Courtesy Lucy Ratcliff

that Thomas had first given to Nannie almost fifty years before was fashioned into a wedding band for their wedding in 1936. Nannie was the maker of dozens of quilts, from bed quilts to doll quilts for her great-granddaughters. A remarkable hand-made legacy, many of these pieces are owned by her family in Arizona.

One of the most popular quilt patterns, and one that was usually made of scraps, is the Log Cabin. Generally constructed on a foundation fabric, the blocks were simple to piece, yet could be arranged into a variety of complex designs. Some variations became popular enough to warrant special names: Barn Raising, Straight Furrow, and Sunshine and Shadow are just a few.

Log Cabin blocks were made of narrow strips building out from a center square. These strips, or "logs," put to good use any long, narrow scraps of fabric. Dating from the mid-nineteenth century, the pattern was made in everything from coarse wool to silks and satins, with cotton the most frequent choice.

A Log Cabin quilt, with blocks arranged in the Sunshine and Shadow variation, has strips hand-sewn around the traditional red center square. The same fabrics are used for the multiple borders, with the darker ones used on the only side

edged with light blocks. The quilting is done in straight lines next to the seam allowances. This was common in Log Cabin quilts, since a more decorative design simply would not have shown well. This quilt was made in the late 1800s in Iowa by Cora Conklin. Cora's daughter, who never married, gave this and other quilts to her best friend, who in turn, gave the quilt to her own daughter.

Another example of the Log Cabin, made in the same era but by an unknown quilter in Missouri, is arranged in the Barn Raising design. The navy-and-white striped fabric gives spontaneity and movement, while the quilt's strong colors and contrast make it a very graphic example of the type. It was pieced by machine onto a foundation of flannel, and although no additional filler was used, alternating strips were hand-quilted. The design is one row off-center, something that shows only when the quilt is flat; on a bed, it would appear to be symmetrical, especially if the longer side were used over the pillows.

For a durable quilt that could be made quickly and used hard, the Log Cabin pattern was a good choice. Interestingly, neither of these quilts show evidence of heavy wear. A variety of fancy fabrics was used in a more elegant version of the Log Cabin. Silk taffetas and satins in an assortment of weaves and

ABOVE: Nannie Catherine Buie Bunkley Crabb, maker of the Stars quilt, was a prolific seamstress and quiltmaker and an amateur photographer.
Courtesy Lucy Ratcliff

LEFT: Stars quilt by Nannie Catherine Buie Bunkley Crabb (1872–1959), Texas, c. 1930; pieced cotton, 61" x 79."
Courtesy Kay Cunningham

prints make up the lighter portions of the design, and the black fabrics show the same variety of textures, with failles and velvets mixed with satins. The quilt is in fragile condition due to the silk content of the fabrics. Black dyes are responsible for the "tendering," or deterioration, of silk; the metal salts used to add body to silk fabrics also contributed to this disintegration. Blocks were split diagonally to create an interesting border, and the various black fabrics form a balanced, striking design, The piece has batting and backing but was not quilted.

Although most quilts were made in blocks, other formats were also used. One was the "strippy" quilt, constructed in vertical rows. Two quiltmakers working near the end of the 1800s chose the same arrangement for their bands of patchwork.

Stacked Bricks is an obvious name for a pattern of offset rectangles. Using a combination of hand and machine sewing, the rectangles were placed diagonally, then joined in rows. In one row, the rectangles were slanted in the opposite direction, possibly a mistake that may have caused the unidentified maker much chagrin.

The wonderful assortment of fabrics indicates a full scrap basket, or at least some access to a variety of prints. Some planning is evident in the distribution of the bright yellow-gold and red fabric among the rows. The border of bright red effectively contains the design.

Taking the same approach as the Stacked Bricks quilt, but with the added interest of redwork embroidery, this Strippy quilt has less distinct vertical lines. Because the same solid fabric was used in the plain rows and to edge the pieced rows, the patchwork appears serrated.

Redwork embroidery, named for the color-fast thread used, became popular after ladies' magazines began promoting naturalistic designs in the early 1880s. Entire quilts were made with redwork blocks. The technique has been used here to decorate the solid rows with designs of cattails, grape leaves, and flowers. The regularity of the designs indicates that a commercial pattern was probably used. The stitchery nicely complements the hard-edged patchwork.

The maker is unknown; the quilt was purchased in Ohio and sent to Arizona as a gift to the present owner.

Throughout the nineteenth century, quilts made for babies and children were simply smaller versions of the patterns then popular for large bed quilts. These little quilts might contain a single, large motif or several scaled-down blocks. The fabrics and colors, however, were the same as their larger counterparts.

With blocks measuring less than six inches, the Birds in Air baby quilt is consistent with this general practice. Made in approximately 1880, the quilt is a mix of hand and machine piecing.

Log Cabin/Sunshine and Shadows quilt by
Cora Conklin, Iowa, c. 1890; pieced cotton,
76" x 86."

Courtesy Jane Ann Juel

Log Cabin/Barn Raising quilt, maker

unknown, Missouri, c. 1880; pieced cotton,

69" x 75."

Courtesy Barbara Nilsen

Log Cabin quilt, maker unknown,
c. 1880; pieced silks, 70" x 70."
Courtesy Elizabeth Rae Landeen

Stacked Bricks quilt, maker unknown,

c. 1900; pieced cotton, 72" x 81."

Collection of Edward C. Flagg

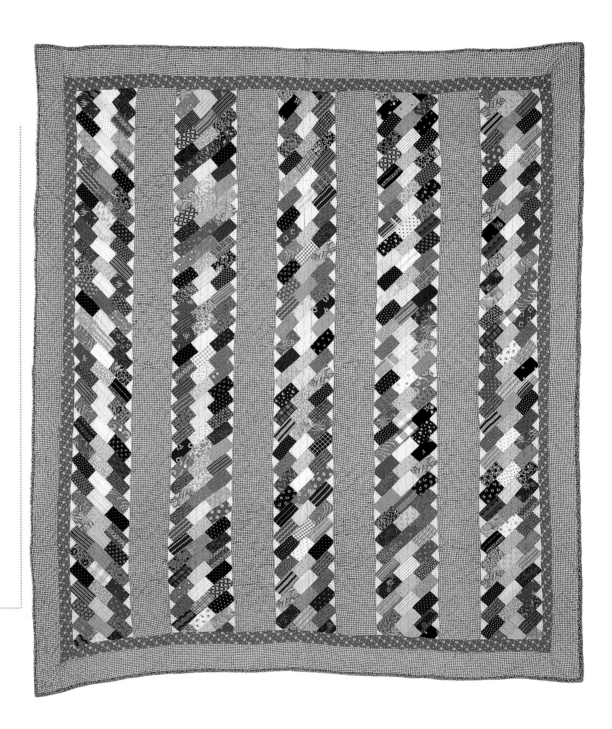

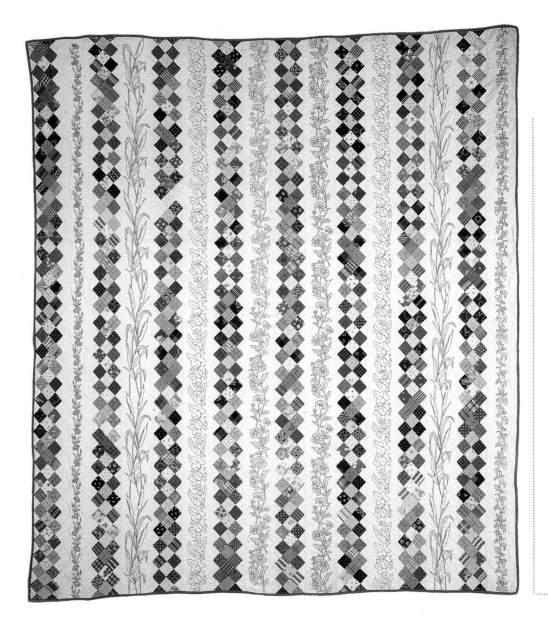

Patchwork quilt with Redwork, maker unknown, Ohio, c. 1900; pieced cotton with embroidery, 75" x 84."
Courtesy Ruth Rhoades

The triangle blocks were alternated with four-patch blocks and framed with plain borders. The prints are typical of the era: red and yellow calicoes mixed with a black-and-white object print. Object prints, sometimes called "conversation prints" because of their comment-causing designs, featured unusual items such as tiny insects, tools, or people. Sporting equipment designs were also common: the Birds in Air quilt shown has a print with little horseshoes and riding crops. The rectangular shape and small size indicates the quilt was intended for use in a cradle or as a doll quilt.

The Victorian style of design, ornate and highly decorative, was also applied to quilts. A popular needlework source of the day, *The Ladies' Manual of Fancy Work*, printed this editorial comment in 1859: "Of the patchwork with calico, I have nothing to say. Valueless indeed must be the time of that person who can find not better use for it than to make ugly counterpanes and quilts of pieces of cotton." Most women continued to use cottons, however, until the fad of the Crazy quilt swept the country in the last decades of the nineteenth century. As silk fabric became more affordable, it was promoted for use in quilts, combined with tiny pieces of velvets, brocades, and other fancy fabrics.

In making Crazy quilts, randomly shaped pieces of fabric were attached to a foundation, and each seam then was covered with embroidery. Motifs were also stitched on any relatively plain areas. For ease in working, most of the quilts were organized into squares, then joined. They usually were not quilted, but rather tacked to a backing fabric. Mainly used for show, most were too small for a bed and were more commonly found artfully draped over furniture in a lady's parlor.

Cornelia Mason Sherwood made her spectacular Crazy quilt in diamond-shaped blocks. She used beautiful materials, mostly silks, in different weaves and textures. An extremely wide variety of decorative stitches adorns the seams; feather stitching, couching, chenille work, and beading are some of the techniques she used. In embroidery and ribbon work are flowers, butterflies, birds, fans, moons, linked rings, and one large web with spider. Consistent with the maker's attention to detail, the backing fabric has been quilted separately from the quilt, then attached.

Cornelia Mason was born in New York state in 1846 and married Stephen Sherwood after moving to Illinois in her early twenties. She made the quilt while living in Joliet, Illinois. The amount of time and talent she lavished on this piece was typical of many Crazy quilts. A poem in the 1891 issue of *The National Stockman and Farmer*, titled "The Crazy Quilt," contains the lines:

Birds in Air quilt, maker unknown,
Pennsylvania, c. 1880; pieced cotton,
25" x 33."

Collection of Bill and Cory Schafer

Oh, the crazy quilt mania, how long will it rave?
And how long will fair women be held as its slave?
And where is the wife who so vauntingly swore
That nothing on earth her affection could smother?
She crept from your side at the chiming of four
And is down in the parlor at work on another.

At the other end of the spectrum is the carefully contained and controlled crazy-type patchwork of Susannah Long Blankenship Melton. This cotton quilt is actually closer in style to a string quilt, which was also built on a foundation, but with stitching covered by the pieces and blocks trimmed to a regular shape. Each block of the strikingly graphic quilt is made up of four squares, except on one side, which has blocks of two squares each. The black sashing, interspersed with the same floral as was used for the border, offers static contrast to the liveliness of the blocks, and the close diagonal quilting line adds texture.

The maker, Susannah Long Blankenship Melton, was born in North Carolina in 1839 and lived her entire life in that state. She married young and was the mother of three or four children when her husband, Hezekiah Blankenship, a Confederate soldier, was killed in the Civil War. She later married W. Landrum

Melton, who also fought in the war, but on the Union side. Susannah, in addition to making quilts, spun her own wool; the thickness of the batting in this quilt may indicate that it was also the work of her hands.

Susannah Melton died in 1926. When her quilts were divided among family members, her great-great-niece in Arizona chose this simple, yet wonderfully graphic, quilt for herself.

WRITTEN IN THREAD

Quilts are often cherished by their maker's families not because of the beauty or worth of the piece but because they represent a record of the person's life. Often they are the family's only ancestral record. Doubly precious, then, are quilts that are signed, sometimes boldly, in large appliquéd letters, but more often discreetly inked or embroidered. Close scrutiny will sometimes reveal a quilted name.

Beyond actual inscriptions, quilts can be carefully "read" to discover the political beliefs, community concerns, and family relationships of the maker. Through choice of pattern, color, or

LEFT: Crazy quilt by Cornelia Mason Sherwood (1846–1909), Illinois, c. 1890; silk and velvet with embroidery, 57" x 63."
Courtesy Ann E. Jeffers

OPPOSITE: Detail, Crazy quilt. An amazing variety of stitches and designs were used in just one portion of the quilt. Chenille-work was combined with gathered fabric flowers; simple outline stitching depicts dragonflies, fans, and sunburst motifs.

symbolism, women recorded their thoughts and feelings. In *Hearts and Hands: The Influence of Women and Quilts on American Society*, author Elaine Hedges observed of nineteenth-century women "...that their stitched fabrics were often the most eloquent records of their lives."

Although denied the vote, many women held strong political beliefs. When a woman featherstitched a colorful silk campaign ribbon onto her Crazy quilt, she may have been casting her vote in the only way she could. One quilt pattern, developed after the 1844 presidential election, was given two names: "Whig's Defeat" and "Democratic Victory." What a quiltmaker called her version of the pattern obviously revealed her political sympathies.

Opinions were also expressed symbolically. A black center was added to the Rose of Sharon design, changing the pattern to Radical Rose in support of the abolition of slavery. Stitched eagles reflect of pride and love of country. Flag quilts, obvious declarations of patriotism, sometimes had further meaning. As Barbara Brackman notes in *Clues in the Calico*, "During the Civil War women incorporating thirty-four stars into their quilts to represent all the states, North and South, were undoubtedly expressing Union sentiments."

Women were usually most concerned with the smaller spheres of home, church, and community, however. These

concerns found an outlet in quiltmaking, as shown by the many quilts made for pastors, needy families, and fundraising. Quilts were either implicitly or explicitly used as a family record, capturing moments in time. As Elaine Hedges observed, "For vast numbers of nineteenth-century women, their needles became their pens and quilts their eminently expressive texts."

One such quilt, rich with images and inscriptions, has quietly carried its message for more than a century. Because the letters were written in thread and the number of other decorative elements was substantial, however, the inscriptions went undiscovered for many years.

Like many of the White Work quilts made between 1800 and 1865, this one is beautifully done, with as many as eleven stitches per inch. Most of the motifs are stuffed or corded. Stylized flowers with large leaves alternate with spread-winged eagles. The head of each eagle is ringed with stars. In the center is quilted a stately house, surrounded by flowers and other small designs. A peacock and cavorting dog are stitched in front of the house. Other motifs include a ram and several snakes; the snake, in keeping with the somewhat patriotic theme, may represent the early slogan, "Don't tread on me."

The family has always called this the "White House" quilt, perhaps as a descriptive name, or one indicating that earlier owners were aware of the inscription under the house that

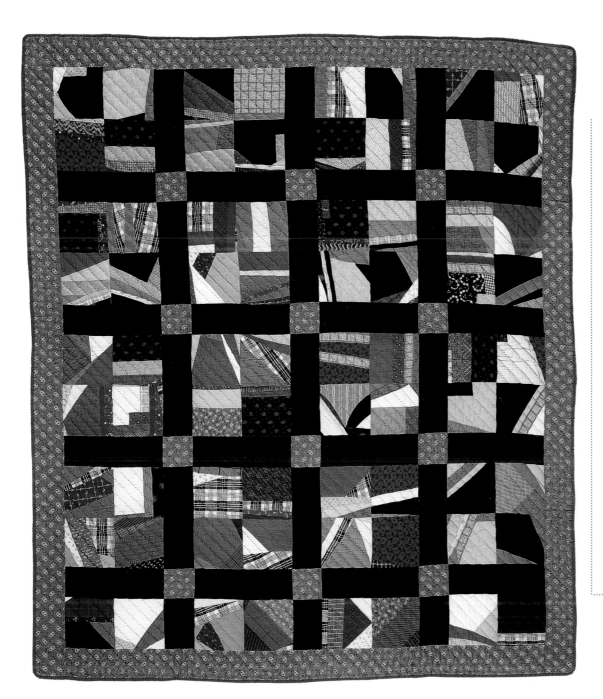

String quilt by Susannah Long Blankenship Melton (1839–1926), North Carolina, c. 1900; pieced cotton, 64" x 73."

Courtesy Lois Melton

reads, "Washington's Headquarters." (It is unclear whether the building represents the presidential White House, but the quilted depiction does resemble the original front, before the North Portico was added in 1829.) Perhaps Washington refers to the city, not the man, since the first president predates the Executive Mansion.

The lettering on the quilt was extremely difficult to decipher because the letters were stitched with both single and double lines, resembling calligraphy. Additionally, stuffing was done between the double lines on only some of the letters. At the top of the quilt there appear the words: "James and Anna Hastings Peoria, Illinois 1844". The original owner lived in Ohio, and briefly in Illinois and Kansas. The family history of the quilt has it that the present owner's grandmother commissioned the quilt during the Civil War, rather late in the era for this type of quilt, although some quilters continued to work in favorite styles long after they were out of fashion. The date of 1844 could be the date of the quilt, or a birth or wedding date; it is unlikely, however, that a quilter would link her name with her husband's on a piece destined for sale.

The nation's centennial stimulated an outpouring of patriotism and pride, which were often manifested in special commemorative quilts. One quilt's purpose is boldly inscribed: the words "Centennial Quilt" are given prominent placement in the center panel of a cotton and silk quilt. The inscription continues, "Aug 29th 1876 Sarah I Smith-Hadley Cambridge, Mass." Hand drawn in India ink is a detailed tree; at the base is the legend, "Under this tree Washington first took command of the American Army." Sarah Hadley was obviously referring to the events of July 1775, when George Washington assumed formal command of the Continental Army, numbering seventeen thousand men, in Cambridge.

The quilt contains more than three thousand one-inch diamonds, arranged in chevrons. It has no batting, but the top is secured to the backing with quilting. The binding is unusual: short lengths of a variety of fabrics were used instead of the more typical single fabric. The quilt was purchased from an antique dealer in New England, so nothing is known about Sarah Smith Hadley beyond her remarkable quilt.

Other quilts commemorate events of a more local nature. This quilt records a disastrous event in the lives of a small community, and the response of a group of enterprising women. In 1909, a fire destroyed the First Presbyterian Church in Beaver City, Nebraska, and nearly engulfed the pastor's manse next door. The pastor's wife, Mrs. J.W. Pressly, and her week-old baby were carried from the home.

ABOVE: Detail, White Work quilt. The amount of quilting and intricacy of the motifs are staggering. Each bird contains more than 50 sections that were individually stuffed.

LEFT: White Work quilt by Anna Hastings, Illinois, 1844; quilted and stuffed cotton, 72" x 82."

Courtesy Judith C. Diehl

Immediately, the women's organization of the church, the Ladies Aid, began a quilt to help offset the cost of rebuilding. Using quilts to make money is a time-honored tradition. Many were sold at auctions or raffled, raising funds for churches, communities, and causes. Among the most interesting of the fundraising quilts are those with signatures: space on the quilt was sold, then the name of the contributor was added in ink or embroidery.

The women of the Ladies Aid constructed a striking blue-and-white Double Nine Patch variation. They charged ten cents for each signature, which was then inked on the plain rectangles. These blocks were joined with a Garden Maze setting, creating a visually dynamic quilt. After it was finished, the women presented it to the Reverend and Mrs. Pressly. Their daughter is now the proud owner of the quilt, a symbol of enterprise and affection.

A good collection of indigo-blue fabrics have been used in the pieced depiction of an everyday object. What is not so obvious is the symbolism behind such a quilt. During the 1800s, several groups worked for temperance or the complete prohibition of alcohol. The most influential of these was the Women's Christian Temperance Union, or W.C.T.U., formed in 1874. With hundreds of thousands of members, it advocated not only temperance but social reforms and women's suffrage. The organization used quilts as banners and for fundraising. Some members, using the group's colors of blue and white, pieced quilts with designs that signified their beliefs.

Drunkard's Path, a pattern with a very crooked design, was frequently made as warning against the dangers of alcohol. The Temperance Goblet was another such pattern, but seldom seen. The blue-pieced goblets perhaps represent the pure beverage of water, but the pattern has the additional symbolism of a bottle turned upside down.

The quilt, dating from the 1870s, is quilted in a design sometimes called the "Baptist Fan," since it was often used by church quilting groups. The semicircular rows of stitching were easy to mark, and a quilt could be finished in a relatively short time.

Brought from Ohio to Arizona, the quilt was purchased by the present owner in 1971. Nothing is known about the maker, except this patchwork record of her philosophy.

Sometimes a more direct approach was taken to declare an affiliation. Emblazoned on the border of a Whig Rose quilt are the words, "Odd Fellows Rose." The International Order of Odd

Centennial quilt by Sarah I. Smith-Hadley, Massachusetts, 1876; pieced cotton and silk with inkwork, 72" x 83."
Collection of William W. Pilcher

Double Nine Patch quilt by the Ladies Aid
of First Presbyterian Church (Beaver City),
Nebraska, 1909; pieced cotton with
embroidery, 77" x 77."
Courtesy Elizabeth Pressly Solso

Goblet quilt, maker unknown, Ohio,

c. 1870; pieced cotton, 77" x 65."

Courtesy Judith L. Rinehart

Fellows, along with other fraternal organizations such as the Masons, flourished in the nineteenth century. The organization's credo of "Friendship, Love, and Truth" is represented by initials and the appliquéd joined links.

The Whig Rose, an elaborate version of the Rose of Sharon design, was done with appliqué and reverse-appliqué techniques.

Several of the leaves have small reverse-appliquéd ovals for buds. In the center block, stems with tiny circles representing grapes were added. The maker not only labelled her quilt but signed it with the letter "S" incorrectly, but consistently, placed backward, in bold, appliquéd letters. The appliqué was done using a combination of stitches: the outside edges were turned and sewn with the usual whipstitch, but the inside edges, more difficult to turn under, were sewn using a buttonhole stitch.

Sarah Munn was born in Ohio in 1832 but moved to Missouri as a child. In 1849, she met her future husband, John Morton Gear, who was on his way to the California gold fields from Delaware, when he married Sarah, "the prettiest girl he had ever seen." In 1852, he continued on to California by way of the Isthmus of Panama, leaving Sarah and their infant daughter in the care of Sarah's mother.

While her husband was gone, Sarah made the Odd Fellows Rose. She entered it into the 1852 Missouri State Fair, where it was awarded first prize. Unable to find his fortune, John returned in 1856. During the four years that he was in California, the family received only two letters and presumed he was dead. After their reunion on his return, five more children were later born to the Gears.

The quilt was inherited by Sarah Gear's daughter, who in turn gave it to a niece because she was named Sarah. The quilt came to Arizona when the present owner, the great-granddaughter of the maker, inherited it, since there was not a Sarah in her generation.

Just as quilts were expressions of beliefs, they also illustrated the attitudes and perceptions of their era. This unusual piece contains nine purchased panels featuring comical depictions of black people in various activities. The center block shows two dancing couples with the words, "The Winners" over their heads. Five other blocks also depict forms of dance, with some obviously meant to be the Cake Walk, a popular folk dance among black people in the nineteenth century. The unknown maker used a variety of embroidery stitches to outline all the clothing of the figures and some of the background details, and tiny pearl buttons were added. The seams between the blocks were decorated with feather stitching. The piece has no batting and is not quilted.

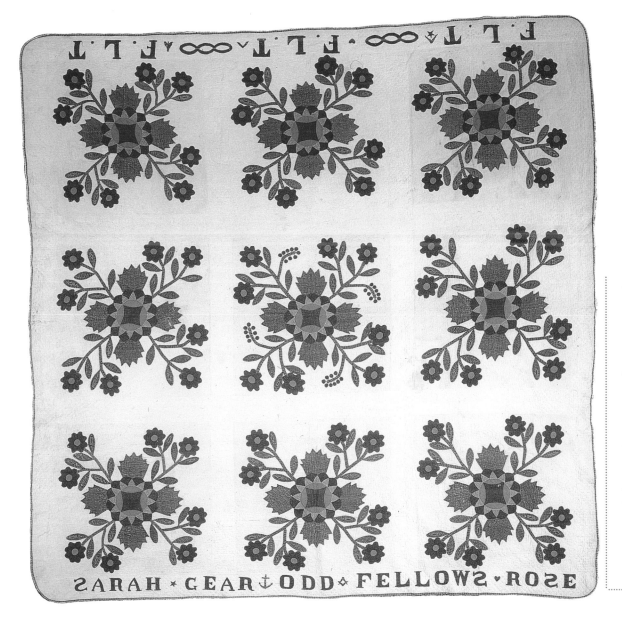

ABOVE: Sarah Munn Gear, with first daughter Eliza May Gear. This daguerro-type was taken around 1854, while Sarah waited for her husband, John, to return from the California gold fields..Eliza May died in 1856, the same year that John Gear returned.

LEFT: Whig Rose (Odd Fellows Rose) quilt by Sarah Munn Gear (1832–1908), Missouri, 1850; appliquéd cotton, 91" x 90."
Courtesy Mrs. Marion W. Askey, Jr.

Home Needlework Magazine, in their January 1900 issue, advertised some of these panels. They were called "Coon Sofa Pillows" and were recommended by the editors: "The coon pillows are the latest addition to the poster family, and it is needless to say the cordial reception they have received is proof of the hearty welcome by needleworkers." The advertisement for "Coon Sofa Pillow Design No. 472B" reads, "The inscription on this pillow, 'If yo' ain't got no money, well yo' needn't come round' is taken from the well known coon song." The panels were tinted in color on plain muslin allowing quick embroidery by needleworkers. Corticelli thread color numbers were listed along with finishing instructions.

Cuesta Benberry, in her article, "White Perceptions of Blacks in Quilts and Related Media," (*Uncoverings*, 1984), noted that derogatory terms such as "coon" or "darky" were so much a part of the national vernacular that respectable magazines easily used such words, even editorially. Quilt historians will recognize this piece as a significant link in the chain of quilts and related items depicting African-Americans as perceived by others.

A unique family record was created by quilting blocks with the stitched handprints of three generations of the Nichols family. Esther Olds Nichols was fifty-eight when she made this small quilt for a granddaughter. On it she traced, then embroidered,

her own hand and the hands of her daughter, son-in-law, and some of her grandchildren. Her block, showing fingers crippled by arthritis, was signed simply "Grandma Jan. 1849," her birthdate. Some of the other blocks, such as her grandson Charlie's, with the year 1894, also have dates. One block, with the words "Melvin 1907 April 1st," shows two tiny baby hands.

Esther Nichols was eighty-five years old at the time of her death in 1934; several others whose hands were represented on the quilt have also died, yet in this quilted keepsake they

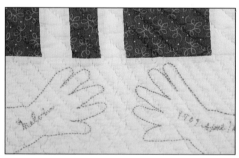

are still joined. The quilt is now owned by the family of Esther Nichols's great-grandson.

A fascinating record of everyday events, and more, could be created in appliqué and quilting. This complex quilt appears to be a calendar of sorts, but also includes perceptive images of the times.

The days of the week are represented in the first ring. Each wedge shows the traditional woman's work week, with Monday represented by laundry on a line; Tuesday, an ironing board;

LEFT: Cake Walk quilt, maker unknown, c. 1900; preprinted cotton with embroidery, 60" x 64."
Courtesy George Motier

OPPOSITE: Detail, Nine Patch Variation quilt. Close-up of border area reveals small handprints and inscription, "Melvin 1909 April 1st."
Courtesy Mary Nichols

and Wednesday, once designated as mending day, a sewing machine. Saturday, the traditional day for baking, is decorated with tiny pies, cakes, and bread. The larger ring was divided into the months of the year. Winter months are shown with ice and snow, a wind-blown tree and kite represent March, a bride and groom occupy the June block, and July is shown with flag and cannons. A classroom scene symbolizes the return to school in September, and the fall months are illustrated by harvest scenes.

Even more remarkable are the quilting designs. The first solid ring is covered with stitched items from the past: log cabin, candlestick, covered wagon, bicycle, horse and buggy, oxen and plow, sailing ship, and water pump. The larger plain ring shows progress with tractor, automobile, train, school bus, and, representing progress to a homemaker, a sewing machine and a mangle, which is a machine to press laundry. The outer corners are filled with images of suns, moons, and stars.

The quilt was part of the estate of Lillian Smith Fordyce, who was born in Illinois in 1884 and lived there until her marriage in 1929. For the next twelve years, until the death of her husband, she lived in Pennsylvania. Then, with a sister, Lillian relocated to California. When Lillian was in her nineties, alone and unable to care for herself, some friends brought her to live in their Arizona home. Lillian died in 1984, a few months before her one-hundreth birthday, and among her belongings was the Calendar quilt. Lillian was an expert seamstress, having worked as a milliner, and certainly could be credited as the creator of the quilt.

Made in the 1930s, the quilt may have been inspired by the Century of Progress quilt contest sponsored by Sears, Roebuck & Company in 1933. Prize money totaled seven thousand, five hundred dollars, and winning quilts were displayed at the Chicago World's Fair. Almost twenty-five thousand quilts illustrating the "Century of Progress" theme were entered in the contest, most of them beautiful renditions of traditional patterns but also among them many original designs, which sought to embody the theme. The Calendar quilt might also have been an entry; the quilted designs illustrate years of technological progress, and the appliquéd designs relate to the passage of time, including the "writing" on the blackboard in the September scene. In embroidery is written: "36,525 days - 100 yr." The quilted initials "C P" in the center of the quilt may stand for Century of Progress. In any case, the maker carefully recorded the world around her in a most remarkable quilt.

ABOVE: Esther Olds Nichols, around the time she stitched her family's handprints on the Nine Patch Variation quilt.

OPPOSITE: Nine Patch Variation quilt by Esther Olds Nichols (1849–1934), Missouri, 1909; pieced cotton with embroidery, 39" x 42."
Courtesy Mary Nichols

With their anonymous domestic art, women expressed their hopes and dreams, shared and preserved memories, and continued both family and quilt traditions. Women then, as today, sought a way to achieve a measure of immortality. Quilts transcended their role as functional objects and became a tie to future generations. Unfortunately a quilt's history, and the family's link to the maker, could be lost in a single generation. The documentation of quilts in Arizona, and the willingness of Arizona quilt owners to share their quilt heritage, will serve to preserve and strengthen those ties.

LEFT: Calendar quilt by Lillian Smith Fordyce (1884–1984), Pennsylvania, 1933; pieced cotton with embroidery, 89" x 94."
Courtesy Victoria Wilkinson

OPPOSITE: Detail, Calendar quilt. Segment representing the month of February shows the amount of detail in the appliqué and embroidery work, as well as the creative use of fabrics.

*L*ike a patchwork quilt, this book has been created through the efforts of a multitude of individuals and organizations. First, our deepest thanks to all the quilt owners and their families, who generously shared their treasured quilts, family stories, and photo albums to make this book a reality.

We thank Arizona historians JoAnn Graham and Karen Smith, Phd., who read early manuscripts to check our facts and gave valuable suggestions. A number of quilt authorities have also helped research specific quilts: Elly Sienkiewicz, Patricia Cox, Bettie Jo Shiell, Nancy Hornback, Mary Evangeline Dillon, Pat Nichols, Cuesta Benberry, Jeannette Lasansky, Gail Andrews-Trechsel.

Our thanks to photographer Al Abrams, Abrams Photo/Graphics, who cheerfully and efficiently photographed more than 100 quilts in just a few days in his studio.

Our thanks to several publishers who gave early advice and encouragement: Bill Fisher, Fisher Books; John and Carolyn Davis, Arizona Lithographers; and Lynn Bailey, Westernlore Press.

It was only through the quilt search and documentation of quilts by the Arizona Quilt Project that this book has been possible, so we must thank all those who supported the project: Major funding (over $2,000) was provided by Western Savings, Grand Canyon Color Lab, the Arizona Quilters Guild, and the Tucson Quilt Guild. We also received grants from the Arizona Humanities Council, the Arizona Commission on the Arts, and the American International Quilt Association.

We thank Linda Callahan, who designed and made the Arizona Quilt Project fundraising quilt, and all those individuals and quilt groups who donated hundreds of quilts to our four Small Quilt Auctions. Our special thanks to auctioneer Tom Martin, who donated his time and learned more than he cared to about quilts, while teaching us about auctions.

We also thank the California Heritage Quilt Project and the Texas Quilt Search for their advice and encouragement.

Our thanks to all the board members who guided the Arizona Quilt Project: Laurene Sinema, President; Audrey Waite, Secretary; Janet Carruth, Treasurer and Book Chairman; Val Benjamin, Quilt Day Coordinator; Carol DeCosmo, Photography, Video and Grants; Penny Fowler, Exhibit Chair and Marketing; Ruth Garrison, Newsletter Editor; Mary Beth Groseta, Oral Histories; June Rector, Judy Schubert, Fundraising and Quilt-Ed; Pam Stevenson, Publicity and Video.

We also thank three former board members who were unable to complete the project: Julie Goosen, Trudy Thompson Rice, and Helen King.

Special thanks to the publisher of Northland Publishing, Bruce Andresen, for his confidence that our vision of a book on Arizona quilts could be transformed into reality; to editor Susan McDonald for her fresh perspective and aid in transforming our text into a final manuscript; and to Northland Editor in Chief Nicky Leach and Art Director David Jenney for their patience with our many questions...and our lengthy list of thank yous.

And finally our thanks to the Arizona Historical Society for co-sponsoring the Arizona Quilt Project. All of the documentation on nearly 3,000 Arizona quilts will be entrusted to their care for future generations of historians.

The Arizona Quilt Project gratefully acknowledges the financial support of these individuals, businesses, and associations.

Arizona Hall of Fame Museum; Arizona Bank; Arizona Commission on the Arts; Arizona Humanities Council; American International Quilt Association; Arizona Quilters Guild; Western Savings and Loan; Arizona State Museum; Linda Aiken; Gwen Albert; Lamora Allen; Catherine Anthony; Sarah Ardus Arizona Cotton Growers; Arizona Department of Library, Archives, and Public Records; Arizona Diamond Jubilee Commission; Arizona Greyhound Foundation; Anna Armstrong; Art's Shutterbug, Cottonwood; BJ Communications, Phoenix; Randy Babcock; Joel Baehr; Margaret Bain; May Baker; Mary W. Ballowe; Val Benjamin; Julia Bentz; Malese M. Black; Joanne Blatt; Joan Boin; Frances Booth by; Kathy Bowers; Cheryl Bradkin; Audrey Brown; Linda Braun; Lynda Brown; Linda Callahan; Linda Campbell; Prue Colo; Janet Carruth; Chandler Nimble Thimbles, AQG; Alice Chew; Anna M. Childs; Joann Christian; Kathryn B. Clark; City of Phoenix, Parks, Recreation & Library Dept.; Louise Coulson; Suzanne Coulter; Carole Collins; Ula Mae Davenport; Boneta Davis; Carole DeCosmo; Terry Dewhurst; Harriet Dolphin; Jo Ann Drake; Claudia Dugan; Nadine Dugan; Patrick Dugan; Evelyn Duncan; Judith Elsley; Evo-Ora Foundation, Tucson; Marjorie Fagan; Marjorie Fetterhoff; Flagstaff Arts & Crafts; Flagstaff High Country Quilters; AQG; Marianne Fons; Zorah Forbes; Memory of Marjorie E. Forsberg; Jeri Fountain; Penny Fowler; Jane Freestone; Helen Young Frost; Karen Servis Funcheon; Darlene Gardner; Agnes Garcia; Ruth Garrison; Gila County Office Supply; Julie Goossen; Grand Canyon Color Labs; Mary Beth Groseta; Debbi Guidi; Marilyn Hamilton; Marilyn Hanutton; Marla Hattabaugh; Betty Hayden; Headquarters West, Cottonwood; Lori Heikkila; Dorothy Heim; Z.V. Hester; Hi Desert Photo, Sierra Vista; John Hokanson; Paula Hokanson; Alice Holmes; Mary Holmes; Carol Hood; Joyce B. Houll; Mary Hoyer; Kitchell Corporation, Phoenix; Immaculate Heart of Mary Church, Page; Imperial LithoGraphics, Phoenix; International Minute Press, Central Avenue, Phoenix; Rhoda Jenison; Wendy L. Johnson; Mrs. J.C. Jones; Leigh Jones; Ruth Cowley Jones; Elnora Jordan; James Jung; Kathryn Jung; Diana Junior, The Portrait Place, Page; Junior League of Phoenix; Kachina Rentals Center, Phoenix; KAET

TV, Channel 8, Phoenix; Sarah Kealy; Helen King; Jack King; Kwik Kopy, Phoenix; Landmark Photo, Sierra Vista; Elizabeth Langsdale; Betty Law; Helen Lawler; Leona Lee; Mary Leist; Sarah Lesperance; Marylynne Lindenfeld; Zada Lines; Marsha Linker; Dorothea Littleton; Courtney Lockridge; Marcia Lorona; Mona Lange McCroskey; Judy McDonough; Mildred McGill; Linda Ross McKillip; Henry McLaughlin; Sue Maglietta; The Marketplace, Cottonwood; Ellen Martin; Eva K. Martin; Mary Martin; Tom Martin; Mesa Cholla Chapter, AQG; Mary Milanese; Monarch Photo; Mountain Bell, Phoenix; Shirley Murdock; National League of American Pen Women; National Quilting Association; Neighbor Lady's Antiques; Bunny Newnham; Mary Nichols; DE Nielsen; Northern Trust Bank of Sun City, Arizona; Ann Novak; Sandy O'Brien; Cindy Taylor Oates; One Hour Photo Express, Sedona; Bonnie Owen; R. Evelyn Perry; Payson Quilting Bees, AQG; Peggy Peck; Sharyn Pennington; Leslie Perez; Phoenix Busy Bees, AQG; Phoenix Crazy Quilters, AQG; Phoenix Night Owls, AQG; Phoenix Sundowner Quilters, AQG; Pine-Strawberry Archaeological and Historical Society; Pine-Strawberry Homemakers Club; Diane Pitchford; Esta Portnoy; Prescott Mountain Top Quilters, AQG; Emmy Procaccino; The Quilt Basket, Tucson; The Quilted Apple, Phoenix; Quilters' Ranch, Tempe; Kathy Garcia-Radspinner; Ramada Inn, Page; Lucy Ratcliff; Madeline Ray; June Rector; Darlene Reid; John Rhodes; Theresa Rhodes; Lovabel Rice; Trudy Thompson Rice; Betty Rieffer; Hazel Riggs; Joan Rogers; Blanche Rowley; Sarah Runnacles; Emma Rulapaugh; Neria Ryder; Connee Sager; St. Paul Womens Guild, Phoenix; Salt River Project; Joyce Schlotzhauer; Judy Schubert; Scottsdale Sunrise Stitchers, AQG; Sedona Red Rock Quilters, AQG; Marjorie Senior; Nancy Shamy; Theora Shelby; Show Low Northland Quilters Guild, AQG; Barbara Sidorakis; Elly Sienkiewicz; Laurene Sinema; Skull Valley Morning Glories, AQG; Southeast Arizona Medical Center; Southwest Gas Foundation; Ernie Startup; Pam Stevenson; Sun City West Calico Cut-ups, AQG; Alice Sundquist; Mary Jean Sweet; Marilyn Swoboda; Maybelle Taylor; Tempe Cactus Patchers, AQG; Virginia Thorne; Betty Lou Tipton; Larry Tretter; Sue Tretter; Tucson Quilters Guild, Inc.; Tucson Roadrunners, AQG; Barbara Uhrig; United Methodist Church of Casa Grande; United Petro; Loretta Vierck; Audrey Waite; Walmart, Sierra Vista; Zelpha Watkins; Shirley Weagant; Jane Wells; Candy Wensing; Mary Jo West; Westcor Partnership, Phoenix;; Betty Wetmore; Esther Whitcher; Mary Lou Williams; Ruth Wright; Yuma Doryels, AQG; Blanche Young; Yuma Regional Medical Center.

The Arizona Quilt Project thanks the following for their time— a priceless gift.

Helen Ackermann; Mary Adjefornks; Vicki Aho; Linda Aiken; Gwen Albert; Sara Albert; Margaret Alberts; Betty Alderman; Fred Alderman; Angie Aleprandini; Jean Alley; Dorothy Anderson; Harriet Anderson ;Ruth Anderson; Betty Andrews; Anna Armstrong: Lois Arnold; Penny Atwell; Norma Ayeman; Aquina Babcock; Betty Babson; Robert Babson; Norma Bailey: Bob Baker; Jean Baker; May Baker; Carol Baldwin; Helen Barnes; Betty Barrow; Kathy Batstone; Barbara Beckner; Helen Beechler; Lou Bencomo; Mary Bencomo; Bob Benjamin; Brie Benjamin; Brock Benjamin; Nell Bennett; Jeanne Bensema; Trudy Bergen; Linda Bigger; Michael Bingham; Natalie Bingham; Jennielee Bishop; Cathy Blair; Nellie Blanton; Joanne Blatt; Lea Boaz; Jan Bolis; Carla Bonifasi; Naomi Boosey; Frances Boothby; Ruth Borchert; Kathleen Bowers; Marian Bowers; Jean Boydston; Linda Braun; Charlotte Brennan: Rita Bridges; Dolores Brock; Jeanette Brooks; Audrey Brown; Betty Brown; Lynda Brown; Melisse Brown; Winifred Brown; Joyce Buchberger; Jeanette Bucholz; Karen Buehler; Marian Butler; Peggy Butler; Kelly Byxbee; Linda Callahan; Sue Calvin; Elaine Cameron: Linda Campbell; Maxine Campbell; Sue Cape; Carol Capono; Wanda Carlock; Kelli Carruth; Kristi Carruth; Melba Case: Dee Cattolica; Maurice Cavenee; Gwyn Chamberlain; Verna Chambers; Teresa Cheney; Anna Childs; Joann Christian; Sandra Christiansen; Ellen Clark: Fran Clark; Carole Collins; Jane Collins; Thelma Connell; Dora Cook; Wilma Cook; Jeanne Copeland; Jane Cordes; Suzanne Coulter; Lynn Crawford; Ann Crutchfield; Amy Cueto; Joyce Cummings; Kay Cunningham; Carolyn Cutbirth; Shirley Cuthbertson; Nancy Brenan Daniel; Cathy Dargel; Boneta Davis; Carolyn Davis; Kitty Deiss; Betty Derivan; Annabelle Dersam; Ruth DeVries; Terry Dewhurst; Mary Lou DeWitt; Rita Dickinson; Linda Dick; Vera Dielner; Inez Dillon; Mary Dillon; Joan Dixon; Dorothy Dodds; Marianna Dodson; Pam Doffek; Betty Dove; Dorothy Drazo; Kay Dries; Elaine Drorbaugh; Jonetta Duey; Maryann Dulski; Anne Dutton; Vicki L. Dwiggins; Heidi Eberenz; Claudia Edgell; Sharon Eisele; Judy Elsley; Cindy Emmett; Ethel Erickson; Nancy Eshelman; Mary Lou Evans; Suzie Evenstad; Marge Fagan; Laurel Fantup; Darcy Falk; Donna Farley; Roy Farley; Eddy Faust; Gloria Fellhaelter; Marjorie Fetterhoff; May Field; Marilyn Files; Rue Fillingham; Nancy Fitzgerald; Peggie Foltz; Retha Foster; Sandy Foster; Valerie Foster; Jeri Fountain; Helen Frost; Tom Frost; Karen Funcheon; Natalie Furrey; Ruth Gale; Daisy Gardner; Darlene Gardner; Sidney Garrison; Janet Garza; Carol Gass; Fran George; Mary Geraci; Anna Giles; Pauline Giles; Martha Gillette; Virginia Gilliland; Betty Girvin; Adona Gladden; Barbara Googe; Vicki Gould; Dorothy Gray; Patty Green; Bonnie Greer; Sally Greiner; Patty Groff; Debbie Guidi; Sylvia Gull; Patricia Hall; Jewell Halla; Betty Hamblin; Marilyn Hamilton; Jean Hamlin; Mildred Hamm; Erma Hansen; Emma Hanshaw; Sheila Hartner; Marla Hattabaugh; Betty Hayden; Lori Heikkila; June Henion; Ellen Henderson; Teri Heser; Valentina Hey; Donna Hicks; Mark Hicks; Margaret Hodson; Crystal Holliday; Alice Holmes; Mary Andra Holmes; Carol Hood; Karen Hopkins; Margaret Hopkins; Nattalee House; Betty Howard; Carolyn Howell; Mary Hoyer; Clorene Hoyt; Pat Hubbard; Millie Hughes; Norma Jeanne Huish; Bunny Humphrey; Mary Hunt; Kay Hunzinger; Tiko Ivakoski; Ann Jeffers; Rhoda Jenison; Shannon Jensen; Barbara Johnson; Jackie Johnson; Lila Johnson; Mary Johnson; Carol Jones;

ACKNOWLEDGMENTS

Kathy Jones; Elnora Jordan; Joy Jung; Karen Kastelic; Bridgett Kearns; Sue Keating; Maggie Keller; Suzy Kemp; Madolyn Kerwin; Helen King; Jack King; Chris Knight; Mona Knight; Ann Korngiebel; Sally Lou Krage; Judy Kuhl; Judy Laing; Marie Lamar; Greta Lancaster; Betty Law; Mary Lenz; Eleanor Lesko; Sarah Lesperance; Joan Lester; Caroline Lewis; Susan Limb; Carol Lines; Marsha Linker; Sandra Lisantti; Eva Marie Lively; Linda Losik; Rosemary Lumpkin; Lynda Lund; Anne Lunt; Ethel Lunt; Karl Lunt; Linda Lunt; Mary McClene; Betty Jo McClure; Janet McCullar; Judy McDonough; Jean MacDougall; Dena McDuff; Millie McEvoy; Debra McKee; Verla McKeeby; Colleen McLyne; Fern McRoy; Leslie Madril; Sue Maglietta; Carole Mahoney; Patrick Mahoney; Betty Mankowski; Vivian Marino; Ellen Martin; Eva Martin; Mary Martin; Terry Mason; Judy Mathis; Lynne Mau; Pauline Maul; Barbara Mead; Carol Meka; Nadine Mello; Betty Merkel; Mary Merkt; Connie Merrell; Fran Meysembourg; Dana Midtun; Carole Miller; Eleanor Miller; Julie Miller; Margaret Milstead; Bonnie Sue Mitchell; Patty Mitchell; Paddy Montgomery; Jim Moody; Vallie Moody; Betty Morgan; Jaime Morton; Shirley Murdock; Bonnie Nanee; Betty Nebeck; Susie Nelson; Gwendolen Nemmers; Betty Neuscheler; Carl Neuscheler; Bunny Newnham; DE Nielsen; Susan Nixon; Ann Novak; Sally Noyes; Sandy O'Brien; Sue O'Connell; Mrs. John O'Leary; Cindy Taylor Oates; Helen Ockwig; Helen Ohlson; Bonnie Owen; Jessica Papoff; Mabyn Peart; Peggy Peck; Venna Peck; Sylvia Pellettieri; Hugh Pendergrass; Minerva Perez; Phyllis Peterson; Carol Pilcher; Diane Pitchford; Karen Plante; Hattie Porter; Virginia Powell; Anne Powers; Mary Price; Emmy Procaccino; Toni Pugliano; Casione Putkin; Peggy Putnam; Jennie Quiroz; Kathy Garcia-Radspinner; Betty Rainy; Madeline Ray; Becky Rector; Cathy Reid; Darlene Reid; Frances Reynolds; Ruth Rhoades; Cheryl Rhodes; Gail Rinegar; Betty A. Roberts; Polly Rosenbaum; Blanche Rowley; Cathie Rudi; Jill Ruggeri; Sarah Runnacles; Emma Rulapaugh; Connee Sager; Ginger Sanchez; Pauline Sanders; Betty Schaeffer; Barbara Schafer; Shelley Sheperd; Willie Schick; Bettelu Schlieper; Jenny Schulte; Karen Scribner; Aleen Searse; Stacie Seeger; Ann Selden; Marjorie H. Senior; Mary Servan; Nancy Shamy; Linda Shaw; Alice Sheets; Johnette Shoberg; Brenda Shriver; Barbara Sidorakis; Dan Sinema; Holly Sinema; Joan Sinema; Mary Martin Sist; Gladys Slack; Bette Smith; Gwyn Smith; Florence Smith; Nancy Smith; Marcia Spark; Marie Spark; Justine Sparks; Charlene Spreke; Gina Spence; Laura Spier; Shirley Springborn; Ernie Startup; Tora Sterregaard; Bill Stevenson; Novella Steward; Judi Stewart; Margaret Straw; Joy Stringham; Virginia Summers; Alice Sundquist; Debbie Sutton; Michael Sutton; Deb Swope; Gene Talbot; Margaret Talbot; Jane Taylor; Maybelle Taylor; Ann Testa; Stephanie Thielke; Sandy Thomas; Barbara Thrapp; Nancy Tokarz; Sue Tretter; Marie Twombly; Lois Van Denventer; Linda Vargason; Meiny Vermaas-van der Heide; Loretta Vierck; Jean Vinyard; Vonnie von Storch; Virginia Wade; Rich Waite; Shawn Waite; Tina Waite; Betta Wakefield; Judith Walker; Anne Wallace; Susan Wallingsford; Dottie Walters; Karen Warner; Jane Watts; Shirley Weagant; Shirley Weik; Mary Welty; Nancy Welch; Maureen Westbrook; Betty Wetmore; Dorothea Whalen; Babe Whipple; Naomi White; Zola L. White; Dawn Whitman; Mary Wilcox; Elaine Wilhelm; Anne Williams; Marjorie Williams; Mary Lou Williams; Brice Willis; Carol Willis; Dorothy Wilson; Gretchen Wilson; Hazel Wilson; Helen Wilson; Keith Wilson; Linda Wilson; Pat Wilson; Mary C. Winn; Barbara Winslow; Mary Ann Winter; Barbara Witwer; Mary Wong; Debi Worrall; Alfia Wright; Betty Wright; Ruth Wright; Marge Wynn; Linda Yantis; Kay Yenerich; Eunice Young

BIBLIOGRAPHY

ARIZONA HISTORY

Andres, Emma. Personal scrapbooks.

Barnes, Will C. *Arizona Place Names*. Tucson: University of Arizona Press, 1988.

Bliss-Hill Collection, Hayden Library Special Collections. Arizona State University.

Bret-Harte, John. *Tucson: Portrait of a Desert Pueblo*. Los Angeles: Windsor Publications, 1988.

Carroll, John Alexander, ed.. *Pioneering in Arizona: The Reminiscences of Emerson Oliver Stratton & Edith Stratton Kitt*. Tucson: Arizona Pioneers' Historical Society,1964: pp.142-143.

Cofer, Iren Cornwall. *The Lunch Tree*. Privately published, 1969.

Corle, Edwin. *The Gila: River of the Southwest*. Lincoln: University of Nebraska Press, 1951.

Dedera, Don. *A Little War of Our Own*. Flagstaff: Northland Press, 1987.

Hughes, Mrs. Samual. "Reminiscences, 1930." *Arizona Historical Review*.

Laetz, Catrien Ross. "San Bernardino Ranch." *Arizona Highways*, October 1986.

Luchetti, Cathy. *Women of the West*. Antelope Island Press, 1982.

Northern Gila County Historical Society. *Rim Country History*. Payson: Rim Country Printery, 1984.

O'Neal, Bill. The Arizona Rangers. Eakin Press, 1987.

Oren, Arnold. "Arizona's Aunt Adaline." *The Arizona Quarterly*, 1946.

Poling-Kempes, Lesley. *The Harvey Girls*. New York: Paragon House, 1989.

Polzer, Charles W., et al. Tucson: Southwestern Mission Research Center, 1986.

Ruland-Thorne, Kate. *Experience Sedona: Legends and Legacies*. Thorne Enterprises, 1989.

Smith, Dean. *Arizona Highways Album: The Road to Statehood*. Phoenix: Arizona Department of Transportation, 1987.

Vonada, Damaire. "Annie Oakley Was More Than a Crack Shot in Petticoats." *Smithsonian Magazine*.

Wells, Reba N. "Cora Viola Howell Slaughter: Southern Arizona Ranchwoman." *The Journal of Arizona History*, Winter 1989.

QUILT HISTORY

Avery, Virginia. "Florence Peto—Renaissance Woman of Mid-Century." *Quilter's Newsletter Magazine* No.118. Leman Publications, 1980 .

Benberry, Cuesta. "White Perceptions of Blacks in Quilts and Related Media". *Uncoverings* 1983. American Quilt Study Group, 1984.

Beyer, Jinny. *The Quilter's Album of Blocks and Borders*. McLean: EPM Publications, 1980.

Bishop, Robert and Elizabeth Safanda. *A Gallery of Amish Quilts*. New York: E.P. Dutton, 1976.

Brackman, Barbara. *Clues in the Calico: A Guide to Identifying and Dating Antique Quilts*. McLean: EPM Publications, 1989.

Brackman, Barbara. "Looking Back at the Great Quilt Contest". *Quilter's Newsletter Magazine* No.156. Leman Publications, 1983.

Cozark, Dorothy. "When the Smoke Cleared". *The Quilt Digest* 5. Quilt Digest Press, 1987.

Ferrero, Pat and Elaine Hedges and Julie Silber. *Hearts and Hands: The Influence of Women and Quilts on American Society*. Quilt Digest Press, 1987.

Fox, Sandi. *Small Endearments: 19th-Century Quilts for Children*. New York: Charles Scribner's Sons, 1985.

Katzenberg, Dena S. *Baltimore Album Quilts*. Baltimore: The Baltimore Museum of Art, 1980.

Lasansky, Jeannette. *In the Heart of Pennsylvania*. Oral Traditions Project, 1985.

Mathieson, Judy. *Mariner's Compass: An American Quilt Classic*. Martinez: C&T Publishing, 1987.

McKendry, Ruth. *Traditional Quilts and Bedcoverings*. New York: Van Nostrand and Reinhold Company, 1979.

Montgomery, Florence. *Printed Textiles: English and American Cotton and Linens, 1700–1850*. New York: Viking Press, 1970.

Orlofsky, Patsy and Myron. *Quilts in America*. New York: McGraw-Hill, 1974.

Peto, Florence. *Historic Quilts*. New York: Chanticleer Press, 1939.

Weissman, Judith Reiter and Wendy Lavitt. *Labors of Love: America's Textiles and Needlework, 1650–1900*. New York: Alfred A. Knopf, 1987.